This book belongs to

_____

Write your name now
and take mastery of the contents!

"Simple and easy. It is very good to learn how to write the letters and connect them. I would definitely recommend this..."
Marina Saleeb, USC student

"It was very explicit. It drills things into your head well. It makes Arabic easy to learn. Simplifies what is generally perceived as a difficult language."
Amy Herrmann, USC student

"I like the creativity of the ways to learn the letters and the integration of the Arabic letters into the pictures. It is a unique and creative way to learn the Arabic Alphabet."
Travis, USC student

"Different. Very creative.
...It's a different and creative way to learn Arabic."
Alex, USC student

"Teaches the alphabet in a novel way, instead of just by rote. It's an easy way to learn the Arabic alphabet that isn't boring."
Otis Clarke, USC student

"I liked the visual, oral combination. By combining the visual of writing it and listening to it, I learn it better. Also, the names (Meem Mung bean sprouts) & Genie would definitely help learners remember. Definitely sticks in mind.
...I would say that it is very accessible, it is easy to learn and remember the letters. Good for learning on your own, too."
Catherine Lyons, USC student

Actually Learn Arabic Letters

A Fun Course That Works--In 3 Weeks

Week 3
Faa' through Yaa'
with five bonus symbols

by Real World Peace

AUTHORITY BOOKS, INC. AUSTIN, TX

Real World Peace is dedicated to promoting pragmatic, sustainable peace in the real world through enabling communication; raising standards of living; creating basic understanding; and giving people the tools they need to run their own lives well. For more information, please go to http://www.realworldpeace.org

Actually Learn Arabic Letters
A Fun Course That Works--In 3 Weeks
Week 3 Faa' through Yaa' *with five bonus symbols*
by Real World Peace

Ⓐ

Published by Authority Books, Inc.
Premiere Edition / First Printing, 2009

Authority Books, Inc.
100 Congress Ave Suite 1100
Austin, TX
78701-4042
United States of America
http://www.authoritybooks.com

ISBN-13: 978-1-886275-04-1
(ISBN-10: 1-886275-04-1)

Go ahead and check out
http://www.authoritybooks.com/arabic.html
for some free stuff that will help you out.

Welcome Back to the final part of an exciting

adventure-- one that will last you well for the rest of your life. You are most of the way through, only a little bit more to go. So far you've already learned the most challenging letters in the Arabic alphabet-- ªein and ghein. You've learned how to pronounce the "dark" sounds of Sod, Dod, Taa', and Zaa'.

And you've even learned about the tanween "n"-sound endings. You've learned so much already! Congratulations!

Now you're ready to start finding out about the final section of the Arabic alphabet. In this book, you'll learn the K, L, M, and N group. You'll learn the last two long vowels, Wow and Yaa', which are actually quite similar to our W (double-u) and Y. And you'll not only learn the h letter haa', but you'll learn a few endings, including a "silent t that looks like an h". You'll see!

After you finish this book, you will have actually learned all of the official letters of the Arabic alphabet, along with all of the important marks, abbreviations, and unusual exceptions. You should be able to write your name in Arabic, and sound out train station names and menu items. You can show off to your friends what you can do.

Lots of people say this is simply the best book on learning Arabic letters--maybe you will too. Because--after you finish this course, and have fun faithfully doing all of the playful exercises, you will achieve mastery over the letters in the Arabic alphabet. You will be able to call each one out by name. You will be able to read each letter, and say its sound. And yes, you will even be able to write the letters yourself.

You will

Actually Learn Arabic Letters!

Acknowledgments

We are grateful to the Parliament of the World's Religions, which is helping to start fulfill the humanitarian dream we have of making education, tolerance, and understanding available for all. Thanks are also due to Philippa Burgess, who has been inspirational in sales and strategy.

Many thanks are due to Imam Jihad Turk, Director of Religious Affairs at the Islamic Center of Southern California, President of the Wilshire Center Interfaith Council, Vice President of the Interreligious Council of Southern California, and Arabic instructor at UCLA, for his kind words of encouragement, and for opening up his Arabic class to checking out the books. Prof. Turk's constant struggle against violence and hatred, and for peace and understanding, serve as a quiet example for all who work with him.

Many thanks are also due to PhD candidate Sarah Ouwayda of the USC Linguistics Department, for laboriously reviewing the text of all three books; for offering countless suggestions and improvements on how the course instructions could be made better; and for kindly opening up her USC Arabic class to testing out the course.

To Sara Al-Faresi, Vice President of Foreign Affairs of the National Union of Kuwaiti Students USA, thank you for believing in the project and for opening up your conference to the group.

To the Arabic students of USC and UCLA who so graciously served as test subjects, gave comments, and kindly allowed their names to be used, we are truly grateful. In alphabetical order: Alex (USC), Otis Clarke (USC), Eddie (UCLA), Amy Herrmann (USC), Catherine Lyons (USC), Kamal Moummad (UCLA), Wendy Radwan (UCLA), Marina Saleeb (USC), and Travis (USC). To the numerous other students who helped out and chose to remain anonymous we also offer a hearty thank you.

Any mistakes that may remain in the book are of course our fault, and not the responsibility of any of these busy commentators who kindly offered their time to advise on sections of early versions.

Mr. Johnny Casey and his base team deserve extra praise for work above and beyond the call of duty, and for providing support during the dark hours.

Exquisite thanks are due to cartoonist Phillip Shrock for his pencils and inks of the funny pictures, and for making the vision real.

Beautiful thanks are due to graphic designer Audrey Snodgrass, for her work on the third version of the covers. Graphic designer Lisa Yu worked tirelessly on much of the intricate writing instructions art work, and provided the gorgeous second edition of the covers. Rachel Hamm, Amber Howell, and Gayle Cantrell were all instrumental in pushing through the production. Great thanks go to Gay Alano for payroll, taxes, and outstanding strategic financial planning. Finally, to all the rest of the Real World Peace and Authority Books teams, many of whom believed in the project enough to sign up for deferred payment--the graphic design team, the writing team, editing, layout and production, the testing team, the marketing group, and the computer support team--hearty thanks is presented. We couldn't have done it without you.

Review Of
A Quick Summary for Smart People

Let's jump right in! Here's a review of the handful of basic facts you need to know about how Arabic works. Maybe you've learned these already, or maybe not. They're still good to review. And don't worry if you don't understand these fully right now. Just run your eyes over them and read these facts for now, and what they actually mean will become clear to you later on.

1. Arabic reads right-to-left on a line. Then the lines go top-to-bottom. After you get used to this, it's no problem.

2. Arabic is written in *script letters* (not BLOCK LETTERS). So they're connected.

3. There are NO Capital Letters.

4. Instead of Capital and small letters, there are four slightly different forms for each letter. These depend on whether the letter is *standing alone* by itself, is *starting* the word, is in the *middle* of the word, or is at the *end* of the word. We will cleverly call these the Stand-Alone Form, the Beginning Form, the Middle Form and the Ending Form, so that you can tell them apart easily. In most cases, many of these will be almost exactly the same inside one letter, so it's no big deal. Certainly it's no worse than, say, having to learn Capital "A" and small "a", I mean, they kind of look like each other but kind of look different. It's the same in Arabic. Usually the Stand-Alone form will be the fanciest, it is kind of like what we think of when we write Capital initials in script. It's the "official" portrait of the letter. Usually the Ending Form will look a lot like the Stand-Alone Form, except of course it has to be connected from the previous letter.
The Beginning Form usually looks like a shorter, more simple version, and the Middle Form often looks like the Beginning Form. You'll see. Remember that the beginning is on the right, and the end of the word is on the left.

A Quick Summary for Smart People (continued)

5. Almost all of the official Arabic letters are **consonants**.

6. There are only three "long" vowels in the official alphabet:
   "aa" (A),   "ii" (or "ee") (y),   and   "uu" (or "oo") (w).

7. There are only three "short" vowels:
   "a" ,   "i" (or "e"),   and   "u" (or "o").

8. Short vowels are written using "accents" (diacritic marks).
   Short vowels are not part of the official alphabet.
   Short vowels are typically **not written** in normal text for adults,
   because everyone knows what they are, anyway.

9. The long vowels are pronounced longer in time than the short vowels.
   That's why they're called "long". And that's why they're written in
   English with double letters. The sound is supposed to be the same, though.

10. Certain irregular forms, such as taa marbuuta, can also count as vowels
    such as "ah". This will all be covered later.

11. There is always a good-sized space **between** words. Just like in English.

12. **Inside** a single word, most letter forms are **connected** to the next letter
    following on the left. However, a few aren't. Like an English script *O*
    (Capital O), the letter finishes, there's a small space, and then the next
    letter has to start up again by itself. It's an **unconnected** letter.
    This will be important.

13. The next letter that follows a "connected letter" is in the Middle Form,
    because it's in the middle of the word. Unless it's on the end, of course.

14. The next letter that follows an "unconnected letter" has to start over and
    be in the *Starting Form*, because it doesn't have any line coming into it.
    Even if it's in the middle of the word. If on the end, use *Stand-Alone Form*.

Actually
Learn Arabic Letters

A Fun Course That Works--In 3 Weeks

Week 3
Faa' through Yaa'
with five bonus symbols

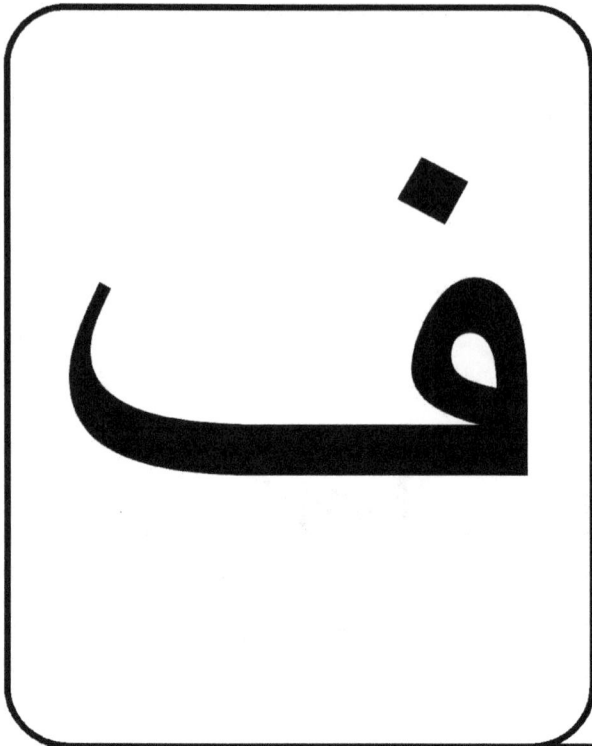

faa'

ف

ف

ف ف ف

f

☾★

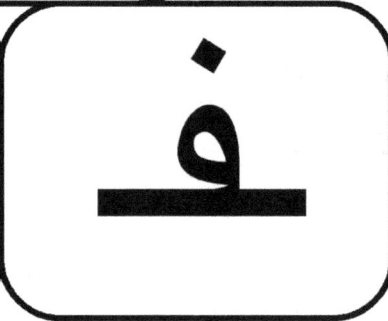

"voiceless labio-dental fricative"

فاء

Faa' sounds like the familiar "f" sound.
It's a light sound that comes from the front of the mouth.

f / ph   *Faa' CONNECTS on the left.*   f

faa'

is Fat Freddy's flying carpet

Fat Freddy flies fast and far
on a flat fantastic flying carpet!
His fearsome attention is firmly fixed on
following one point in his furry head.

Helpful Hints

Fat Freddy has a big stomach that points to the left, and slightly down. His back is straight, though. Note that the one dot for his head comes on top of his stomach, but leans forward very slightly, for both the Stand-Alone and Ending forms. Don't disconnect it so that his head is hanging out over his carpet, though!

Fat Freddy's flying carpet stays flat _on_ the line, whereas, in the next letter, the Queen's beckoning arm goes way **below** the line in a familiar bowl-shaped curve. The Beginning and Middle forms are almost exactly the same, though, with just one or two dots.

Fat Freddy's body is roughly triangular. His stomach hangs outwards and down, his shoulders point up, and his ankles form a hard corner with his stomach line. It's not just a round circle.

Now You Sketch It--Doodles!

How To Write It

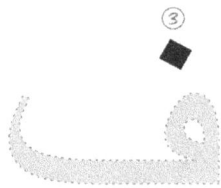

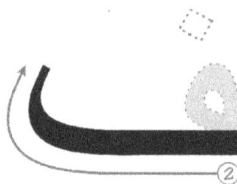

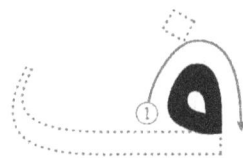

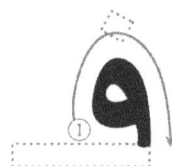

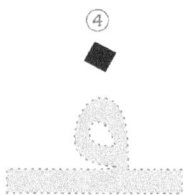

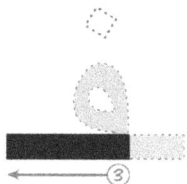

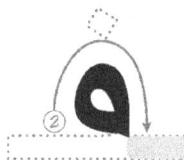

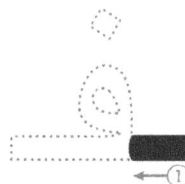

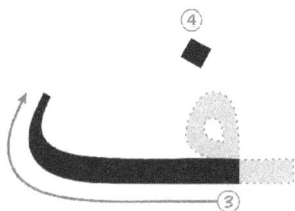

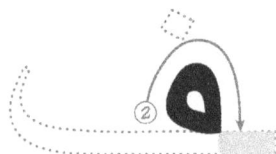

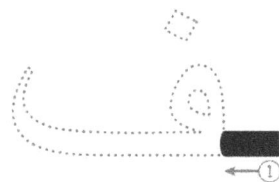

ف

ـف

ـفـ

فـ

Writing Suggestions

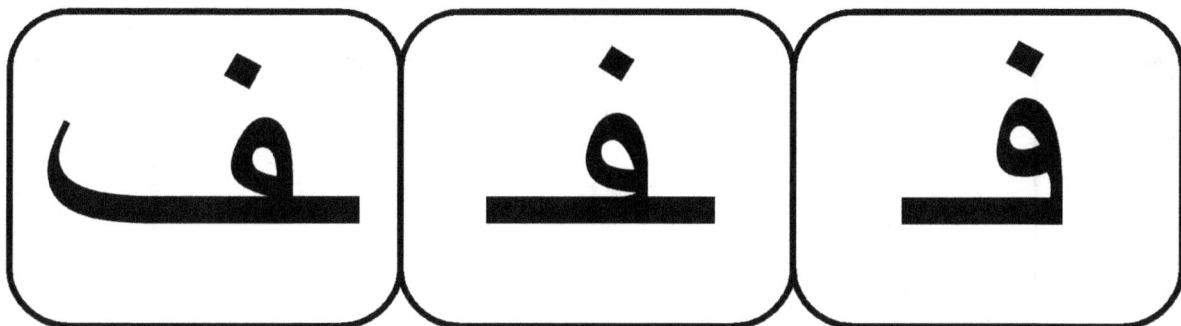

Stand-Alone Form
1. Starting just above the line, draw a fat loop clockwise. Short, no legs.
2. Make a hard corner, then draw the flying carpet. It is quite long.
The flying carpet is **flat**, until the curl at the end, and it is *on the line*.
3. Come back and put a single dot above for his head. Slightly in front.

Beginning Form
1. Starting one-third of the way up, draw a fat loop clockwise, two-thirds
of the way up. It looks like a short "9". Freddy has legs this time.
2. Make a hard corner, then continue straight on the line on to the next.
3. Sometime afterwards, come back and put a dot in for his head.
This time the dot is directly above his body.

Middle Form
1. Come in on the line connected from the previous letter.
2. Pick up your pen and put it slightly above the line. Draw a fat loop
clockwise. You can see his ankles, but no long legs this time.
3. Make a hard corner, and continue on the line to the next letter.
4. Sometime later come back and dot the head, directly over the body.

Ending Form
1. Coming in on the line from the previous connected letter.
2. Draw a fat loop clockwise. You can't see his ankles this time.
3. Make a hard corner, then continue on flat on the line. End curves up.
4. The head is slightly in front of the body for the ending form.
His head does not touch his body, but he's a polar cat thing, not a giraffe.

Writing Practice

Say the name of the letter, and make its sound,
each time you write the letter.

Writing Practice

Now put them together.
Remember to keep each letter
separate in your mind.

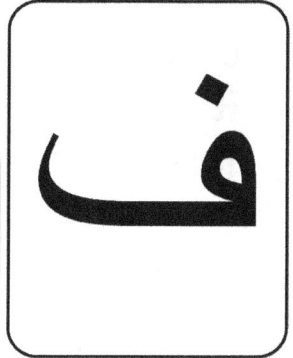

ف	ـف	ـفـ	فـ

Know The Difference!

Qaaf has TWO dots.
It's the two-quote queen's Custom Comfortable Crown.

ق

Baa' has no loop,
and its one dot is on the Baattom.

ب

Wow points downwards
and has no dots at all.
It also never connects on the left.

و

Ghayn has a tight, raised, triangular loop,
not rounded.

غ

Daad has a flat, sand-Dune loop,
with a following little hill-crest.

ض

Zaay and Noon have no loop at all.

ن ز

Reading Practice

في

فطر

فطر	في
r T f	y f
fiTr	fee
mushroom	in, at

فأر

فلفل

فلفل	فأر
L f L f	r 'A f
fulful	faa'r
peppers	mouse, rat

غولف

فشار

فشار	غولف
f A sh f	f L w gh
fushaar	ghoolf
popcorn	golf

Qof

"uvular stop" قاف

Qof (or "qaaf") is pronounced like a dark, emphatic "k" that comes from deep down in the throat. It is a normal "k" that does not have the scrape in it that Khaa's "kh" does. The dark "k" is found in English as the first sound in "cough", "custom", or "curtains". Try to move it back and down, coming from as deep in your throat as possible. It is **NOT** followed by a secret w sound, as English "q" normally is ("quick" should be spelled "kwik"). Just use the "k" sound in "cough".

q / 8 / 9 / 2   *Qof CONNECTS on the left.*   q, Q

Qof

is Cough, the Two-Quote Queen

cough cough
"I want two quotes!"
quoth the Queen.

Cough, the *two-quote* queen's
Constant quest for Comfortable
quality *dark* Custom Curving
Cushion Curtains.
Cough! Cough!

Helpful Hints

Qaaf probably should have been spelled in English using "c", but every-one uses a "Q" now, so we're out of luck. With the exception of quay, quiche, and quoit, most "q" words in English have a secret "w" sound after the "k". Drop this, we don't want it. Just remember that **"The Queen prefers Quiche to be Cut"**, and you'll turn your q's into C's [dark k's] in your mind as well.

Qaaf's "c" is a "k" that comes from the back of the throat. First say "kiss-kiss-kiss". Notice how the "k" sound is light and high-pitched. All the action is coming from the front of your mouth, between your teeth. Now say "crumble" or "curtain". Notice how the "c" sound is dark and low-pitched, and comes from the back of your throat. Although we would call both of these "k" sounds, in Arabic the dark K pronounced all the way in the back of the throat is considered to be different from the "k" sound. It's called a Qof sound, and is spelled "Q".

Because you are using the back part of your tongue to hit the back part of your mouth, you could in fact say the dark k with your mouth completely open. Say "Cut-cut-cut". Now open your mouth all the way, and only say the first part--"cu-cu-cu". Notice how your tongue is squeezing the back of your throat to make the "k" sound. Close your mouth, and you can still make this sound. Now that you know what to look for, swap back and forth between "kiss" in the front of your mouth, and "cut" in the back of your mouth--"Kiss -- cut -- kiss -- cut -- kiss -- cut". They really are different! Now that you're doing it, you can tell the difference, too!

Now You Sketch It--Doodles!

How To Write It

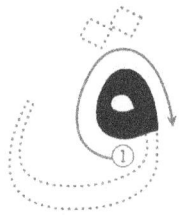

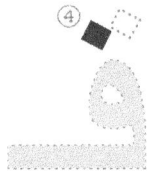

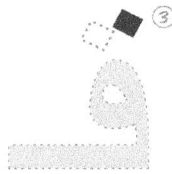

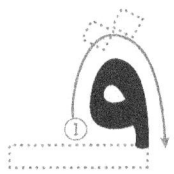

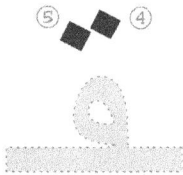

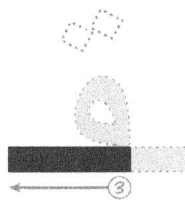

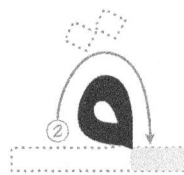

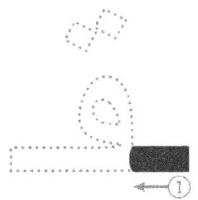

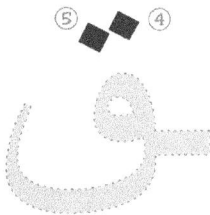

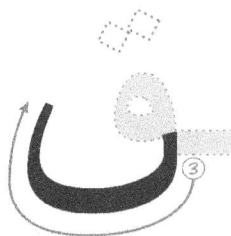

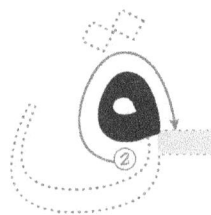

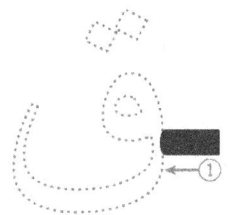

Writing Suggestions

ﻕ ﻘ ﻗ

Stand-Alone Form
1. Start on the line. Draw a fat three-sided loop that comes clockwise.
2. Continue on down below the line. Draw a fat bowl . The end comes up slightly above the line, and tapers off gracefully.
3. Make one dot directly above the head, then the second dot beside it to the left. The dots float high, it's a tall crown.

Beginning Form
1. Starting one-third of the way up, draw a fat loop two-thirds of the way up. The loop is above the line, with a flat back like a short "9".
2. Make a hard corner. Continue on flat on the line to the next letter.
3. Sometime later come back and put in two dots centered on top.

Middle Form
1. Come in on the line from the previous connected letter.
2. Draw a fat loop clockwise.
3. Make a hard corner, then continue flat on the line to the next letter.
4. Come back later for two dots centered above. They float quite high.

Ending Form
1. Come in on the line from the previous connected letter.
2. Pick up your pen and draw a fat loop, starting just above the line.
3. Continue downwards swooping into a large bowl shape below the line. The tail of the bowl, the queen's hand, ends up above the line.
4. The first dot is centered above her head, the next dot beside. High.

Writing Practice

Say the name of the letter, and make its sound,
each time you write the letter.

Writing Practice

Now put them together.
Remember to keep each letter
separate in your mind.

ـق	ـقـ	قـ	ق

Know The Difference!

Faa' has only one dot. It's Fat Freddy's head, as he stands on his Fantastic Flying carpet.	ف
taa' MaRbuuTah unconnected, the feminine special-crowned tiny hummingbird egg, is stand-alone. (Aah! How cute!)	ة
Ghein has only one dot and has a triangular loop.	غ
taa' has no loop. The final form is also flat, like a toboggin, not curved.	ـت ت
taa' maRbuuTah connected on the right looks like a feminine horsey saying "Aah". It only comes at the end of words, and is bent forward, with no curving arm following.	ـة
Wow, the Wide White toWel, does not have any dots at all. It descends below the line in a short curve.	و

Reading Practice

قادَ

a d A Q
Qaada
to drive; to lead

قد

d Q
Qad
[have done]; already;
may, might

قرد

d r Q
Qird
monkey

قبل

L b Q
Qabbala
to kiss

القدس

s d Q L A
al-Quds
[the] Jerusalem

طبق

Q b T
TabaQ
dish (plate; food)

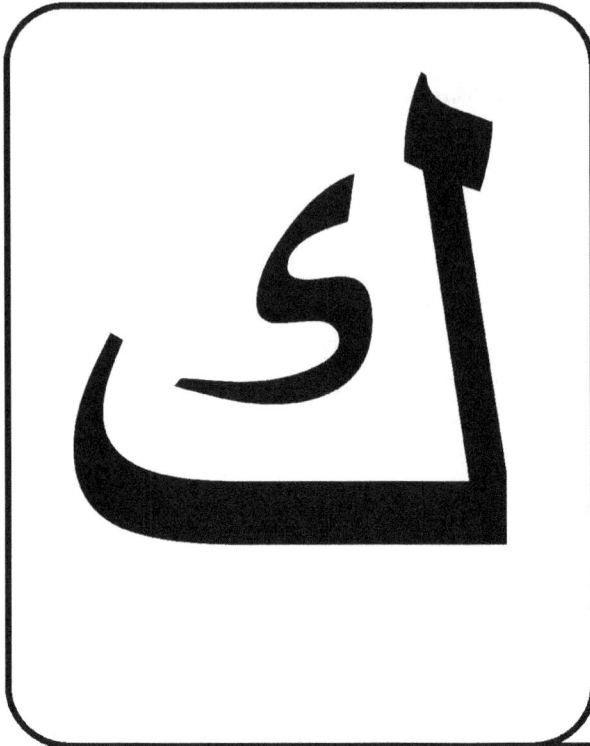

kaaf

ك

k

كـ ـكـ ـك

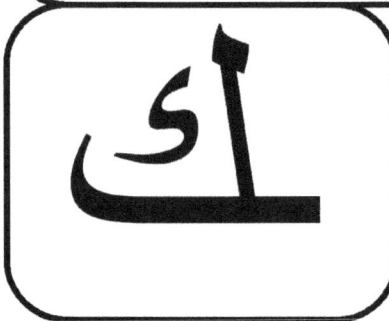

"voiceless velar stop"

كاف

kaaf is pronounced just like the familiar light "k" of "kiss". It comes from the front of the mouth.

k   *kaaf CONNECTS on the left.*   k

kaaf

is Kris Kringle's ski boots

Kris Kringle's
calf-high
king-sized
ski boots.
oh...Kay!!

Helpful Hints

Kaaf has two major forms--the flying Kris Kringle on his skiis, for the beginning and middle forms, and the huge king-sized ski boot, for the ending and stand-alone forms.

The ski boot is one of the largest letters--it is as tall as an 'aalif or a Taa', and almost as wide as a faa'. The little sign inside the ski boot is always written as an S, never as a Z. If you wrote it backwards like a Z, the elf boot wouldn't make any sense any more, and you wouldn't have something going out to the toe of the boot. Remember that **there's an "S" in "ski" boot.**

Kris Kringle himself is actually formed from *two* strokes. They don't match up perfectly. That's how you can see his face and his beard, which give a rough spot on the letter.

The light "k" of kaaf (front of the mouth, "calf") is different from the dark "k" of Qof (back of the throat, "cough"). Make sure you can tell how.

Now You Sketch It--Doodles!

How To Write It

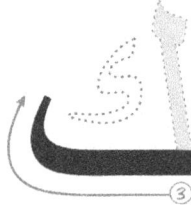

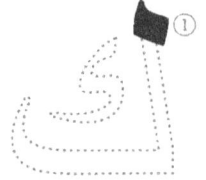

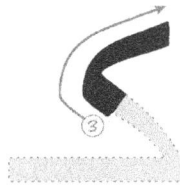

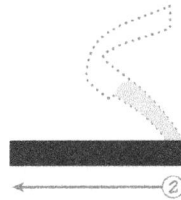

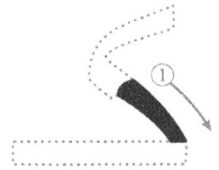

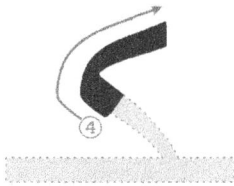

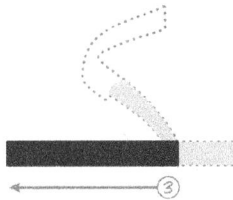

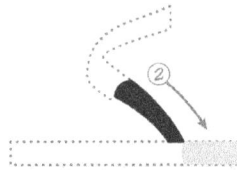

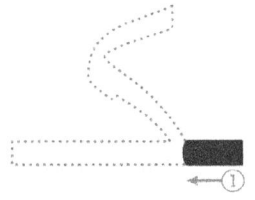

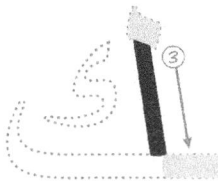

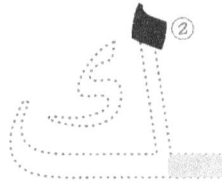

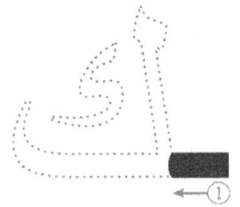

Writing Suggestions

Stand-Alone Form

1. Draw a little tick mark, a serif, at the top, a full height above the line.
2. Draw the back of the ski boot coming straight down onto the line.
3. Draw the bottom of the ski boot on the line. The toe curls up (elves).
4. Draw a fancy S-shaped flat curve that almost touches the top of the boot on the right, and almost touches the tip of the toe on the left.

Beginning Form

1. Start one-third of the way up and draw Kris's body, straight, slanting.
2. Make a hard corner and draw the skis on the line, to the next letter.
3. Sometime later come back and, starting with Kris's head, draw his head then a corner, and his long ski cap. The results look like a K's legs.

Middle Form

1. Come in on the line from the previous connected letter.
2. Pick up the pen and jump one-third up above the line. Draw a slanting line straight backwards to meet the previous one.
3. Make a hard corner. Continue flat on the line on to the next letter.
4. Sometime later come back and start with Kris's head, then draw his long ski cap. The end of the cap is just above his ankles, not longer.

Ending Form

1. You come in briefly from the previous connected letter.
2. Pick up the pen and make a tick mark a full height above the line.
3. Follow on as with the Stand-Alone form.

Writing Practice

Say the name of the letter, and make its sound,
each time you write the letter.

Writing Practice

Now put them together.
Remember to keep each letter
separate in your mind.

كـی	کـک	کـ	لـك

Know The Difference!

Laam has no ski-boot buckles in the middle.	لـ ل
Alif is not connected on the left side.	ـا
Daal is short, and it has no flying elf-hat. Daal is always unconnected on the left. And of course it has the Dallas Duck tail.	ـد
Final Laam-Alif looks like a singing eeL from L.A. LeAning on a LAmp-post.	ـلا
Taa' has the Tall, Tall Tower beside the hill.	ـط
Stand-alone Laam-Alif looks like an eeL singing "LA".	لا

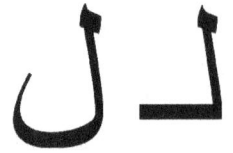

Reading Practice

كبير	كعك
r y b k	k ᵃ k
kabeer	kaᵃk
big	cake(s)

ضحك	فاكس
k H D	s k A f
DaHk	faaks
laugh	fax

كثير	كورس
r y th k	s r w k
katheer	kooras
many	chorus

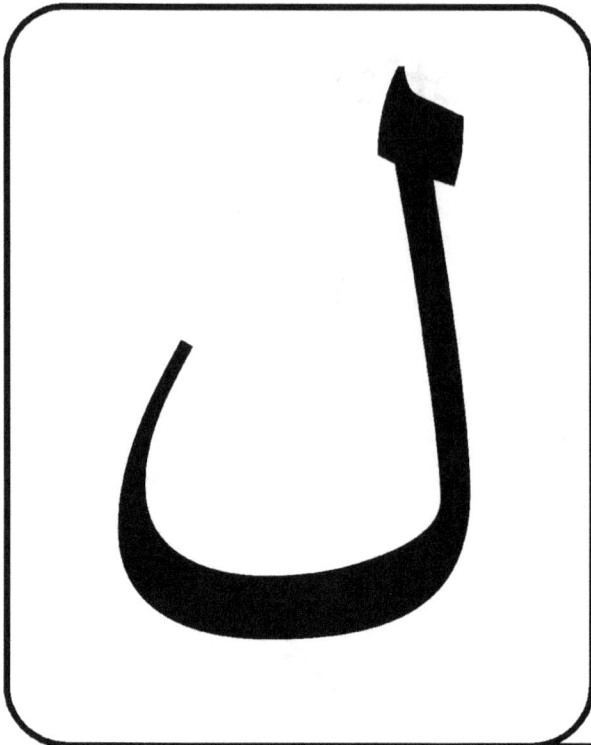

laam

ل

ل

لـ

ــد

ــلـ

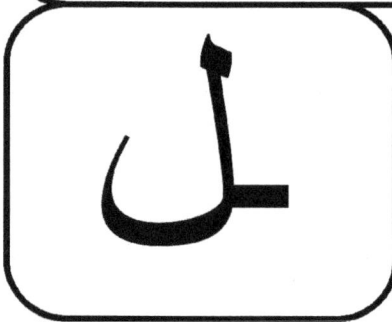

"alveolar lateral"

لم

Laam is pronounced like the familiar "L".

l   *Laam CONNECTS on the left.*   l

laam

is the Electric Lamp Eel

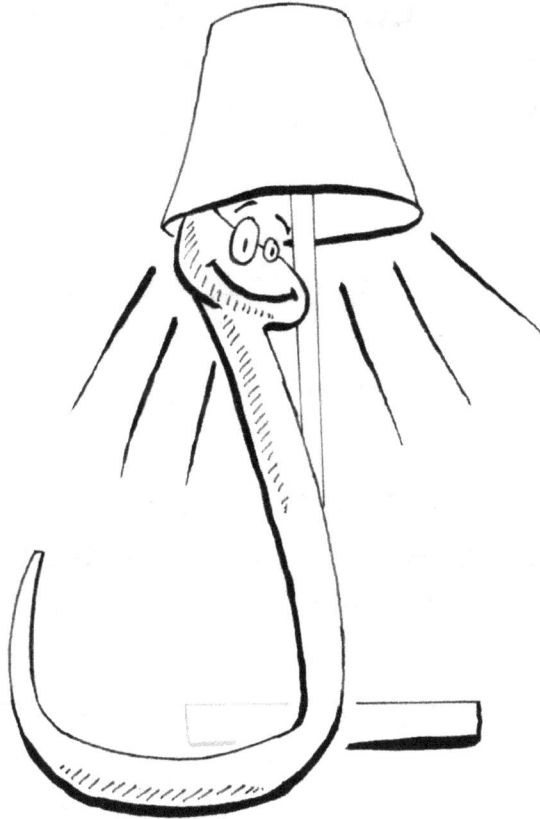

Laam is Larry Leel
The Electric Lamp Eel--
He likes light to shine bright on his lid!
This *backwards Eel* leans
On a lamppost and dreams
Of the laughter and life he will lead.____

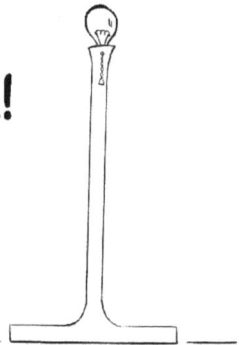

Helpful Hints

Laam looks like a **backwards** L. Since Arabic writes from right to left, the L faces to the Left as well. This makes sense. Notice that the ending form gets fancy and rounded.

The Greek name for L is "Lamda" (Λ). It looks like an up-side-down L, not a backwards L. People were still trying to make up their minds in which direction to draw L for a long time. Notice that the word "Lamda" starts with "Laam".

Laam comes in two forms, the looping eel/fishhook for the ending or stand-alone forms, and the connected vertical lamppost for the beginning and middle forms. Because the lamppost sits on the ground, it is connected on **both** the left and the right. And it has a hard right-angle at the bottom. This is different from the 'aalif space-rocket, which is *not* connected on the left, and which has a rounded corner at the bottom when it's used in the middle or at the end.

L will usually have a little serif, a bump, up at the top, in most fonts. This also helps to distinguish it from 'aalif, which has no bump.

Now You Sketch It--Doodles!

How To Write It

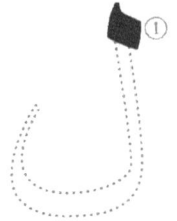

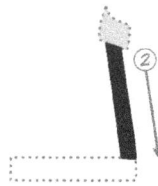

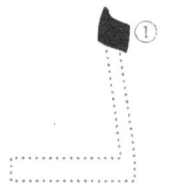

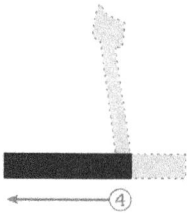

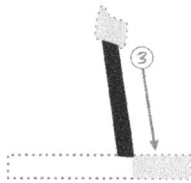

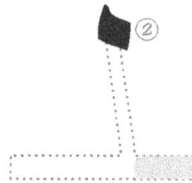

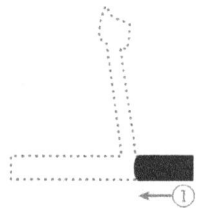

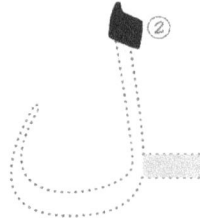

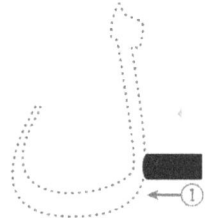

Writing Suggestions

Stand-Alone Form
1. Start a full height above the line. Make a tick mark, a serif.
2. Make a large, elegant, looping rounded fish-hook eeL shape. Come straight down until you reach the line. Then form a shallow bowl shape just slightly below the line, not very deep. The tail of the eel comes up high, almost one-third of the way back up above the line.

Beginning Form
1. Make a tick mark, a serif, a full height above the line.
2. Come down straight onto the line, a full height.
3. Make a hard corner. Continue on the line flat, on to the next letter.
It is a backwards L. It connects and so is quite different from the rocket ship of 'Aalif, which stands alone in a field all by itself, unconnected.

Middle Form
1. Come in from the previous connected letter on the line.
2. Pick up the pen. Make a tick mark, a **serif**, directly above, a full height.
3. Make a full line straight **down**, to a **hard corner**. (Note this is quite different from a Middle 'Aalif, which goes **up** from a **rounded corner**.)
4. Continue on the line flat, on **connected** to the next letter. This forms a backwards L. (Note the Middle 'Aalif is **unconnected**.)

Ending Form
1. Come in from the previous connected letter on the line.
2. Pick up the pen. Make a serif mark a full height above the line.
3. Make a looping fish-hook shape that extends slightly below the line.

Writing Practice

Say the name of the letter, and make its sound,
each time you write the letter.

Writing Practice

Now put them together.
Remember to keep each letter
separate in your mind.

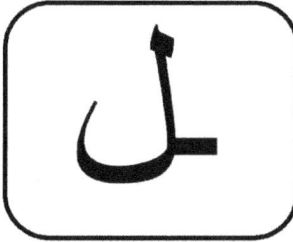

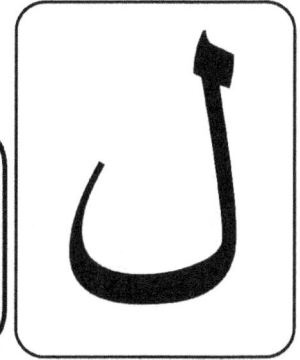

ﻝ

ﻝ ﻟ ﺪ

Know The Difference!

Final or stand-alone Kaaf
is wider, square, has sKi bucKles,
and is not shaped like a fishhook eel.

ك

Middle or Final Alif
has no connection on the left.

ﻞ

Stand-alone or initial Alif
also has no connection on the left.

ا

Laam-Alif is in fact a Laam,
followed by a singing eeL from L.A.,
a contraction for Laam + Alif together.

ﻼ

Taa' has the Tall, Tall Tower
beside the hill.

ط

Stand-alone Laam-Alif is in fact a Laam,
followed by an Alif, it's a contraction.
It's a singing eel from L.A.

لا

Reading Practice

ل

L
li
to; for; so that

لي

y L
lee
my, mine, I have

لتر

r t L
litr
liter

ليس

s y L
laysa
no (nouns, adjectives)

لطيف

f y T L
laTeef
kind

لعل

L ᵃ L
laᵃalla
perhaps

meem

m

  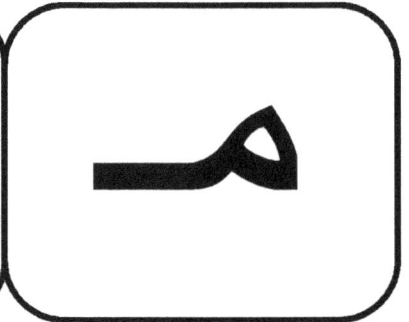

"bilabial nasal"

ميم

Meem sounds like the familiar "m".

m　　　　*Meem CONNECTS on the left.*　　　　m

meem

is the Mighty Mean Mung beans

Mom's mini meany Mung beany sprouts.
Thinking mean thoughts keeps them small,
Most will never grow at all!
Mean Mung Beans, don't mumble so
Dream great dreams, and you will grow!
Open up your heart and Mind,
Life is Meem-'rable when you're kind.
From the Mung beans' growing surge,
Mighty beanstalks May eMerge.

Helpful Hints

Meem has a number of different forms, depending on the type font. Sometimes the ending and the stand-alone forms will have a closed loop, like a mung bean. Sometimes they will have an open leaf sticking out. It depends on who drew the font.

The ending form looks a bit like the Greek letter "mu" (μ), which also stands for "M". Note the part going below the line on the left, attached to a loop in the middle.

The Mung beans are round bumpy circles, but they still sit on the line. The round beans are in the beginning and middle forms. This is different from the horsey face of haa' and taa'-marbuuta, which sticks up above the line and only comes at the end.

Now You Sketch It--Doodles!

How To Write It

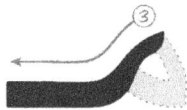

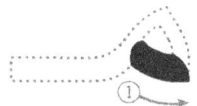

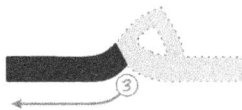

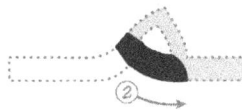

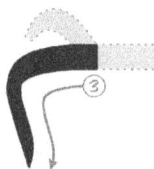

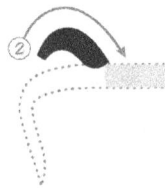

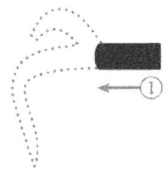

Writing Suggestions

Stand-Alone Form
1. Start the Meem ahead of where you want it, and slightly above the line. The Stand-Alone Form is going to move in a clockwise direction. Usually the stand-alone form is open, although sometimes it can be a closed loop. Draw an arch, over and onto the line.
2. Continue on the line to draw the "ground". Then smoothly turn downwards and draw the "root". The root is a sweeping curve that ends up pointing downwards.

Beginning Form
1. The Beginning Form is a triangular bean that goes counter-clockwise. Start just barely above the line , and draw a short stroke coming down onto the line.
2. Continue around going upwards., without lifting pen from paper.
3. Close the loop, and continue on. The loop is small and rounded.

Middle Form
1. Coing in from the right, make a corner and go up and over.
2. Continue clockwise to close the loop and make a small bean circle.
3. Lift your pen. Pick up from the corner and continue on to the next letter.

Ending Form
1. You're coming in from the right, on the line.
2. Pick up your pen. Jump ahead. Draw an arc down to the line, it's the leaf/steam.
3. Draw a flat part for the ground, then a swooping curve for the root. End up pointed straight downwards.

Writing Practice

Say the name of the letter, and make its sound,
each time you write the letter.

Writing Practice

Now put them together.
Remember to keep each letter
separate in your mind.

حـ	ـمـ	ـم	م

Know The Difference!

Middle Faa' or Qaaf has a loop that sits on top of the line. It's a stomach or a head scarf that points off to the left, and has one or two dots on top.

ف
قـ

Beginning ᵃayn has a singing lamb's mouth that points off to the right.

عـ

Middle ᵃayn has a lamb's ribbon that is flat on top. And final ᵃayn loops around, back to the right. They both have tiny loops, but they're small and triangular.

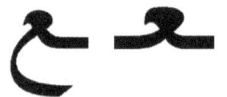

ـعـ ـع

Ending haa' is shaped like a Happy Horse. The distinctive Horsey shape is different from a bean sprout, and has no root.

ـه

Haa' the Hot Hot Hero Hat is long and curving, like a Hot pepper. The Hot Hat also has no root.

حـ
ـح

Wow the Wide White toWel opens doWnWards and to the left.

و

Reading Practice

جميل

L y m j
jameel
beautiful

امام

m A m A
aamaam
in front

حلم

m L H
Hilm
dream

جمل

L m j
jamal
camel

ممّا

A 2 m m
mimmaa
than

مسلم

m L s m
muslim
Muslim

أمن

n m 'A
amn
Peace

ممتع

[a] t m m
mumti[a]
enjoyable

noon

n

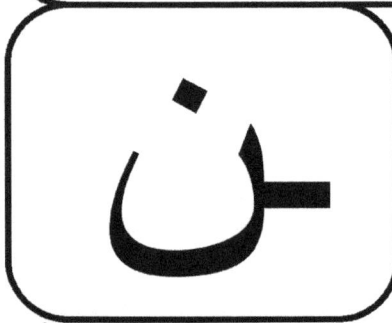

"alveolar nasal"

نون

Noon sounds like the familiar "n".

n   *Noon CONNECTS on the left.*   n

noon

is Nice Norman the Genie

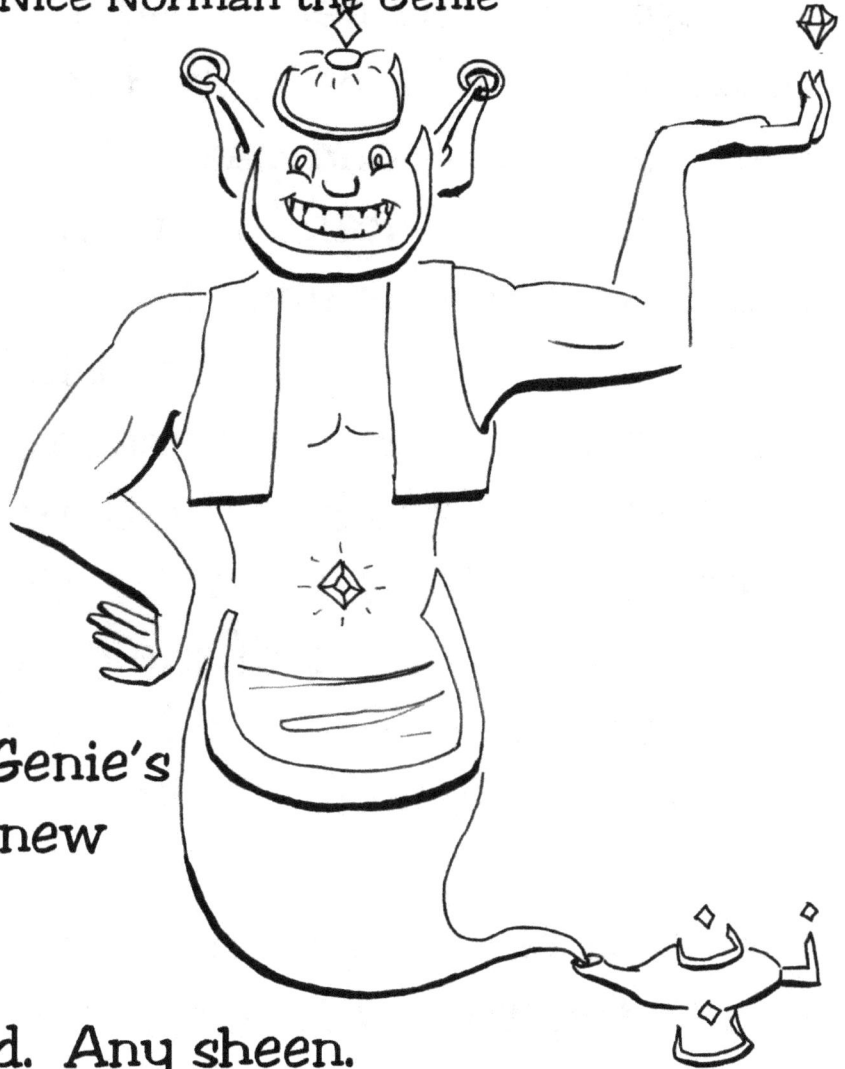

No one knows
Nice Norman Genie's
navel needs a new
nice, clean
inner green
single diamond. Any sheen.
One for his belly or one o'er his nails.
Any one diamond, at Noon, never fails.

Helpful Hints

The spike on the beginning and middle forms of noon is the same spike that is used for baa', taa', thaa', and yaa'. The large bowl on the ending and stand-alone forms is the same bowl that is used for seen, sheen, Saad, and Daad. Because it is not linked with extra stuff in front of it--seen has the glasses, and Saad has the Sand dune, but noon has nothing in front-- it's easy to tell it's noon. And none of the other bowl forms have a dot over the *bowl*--Daad has a single dot, but it's over the *Dune*.

For some reason, this run of consonants all comes together. English has K, L, M, and N. Greek has Kappa, Lamda, Mu, and Nu. And Arabic has Kaa', Laam, Meem, and Noon. It makes it easy to remember this segment.

Now You Sketch It--Doodles!

How To Write It

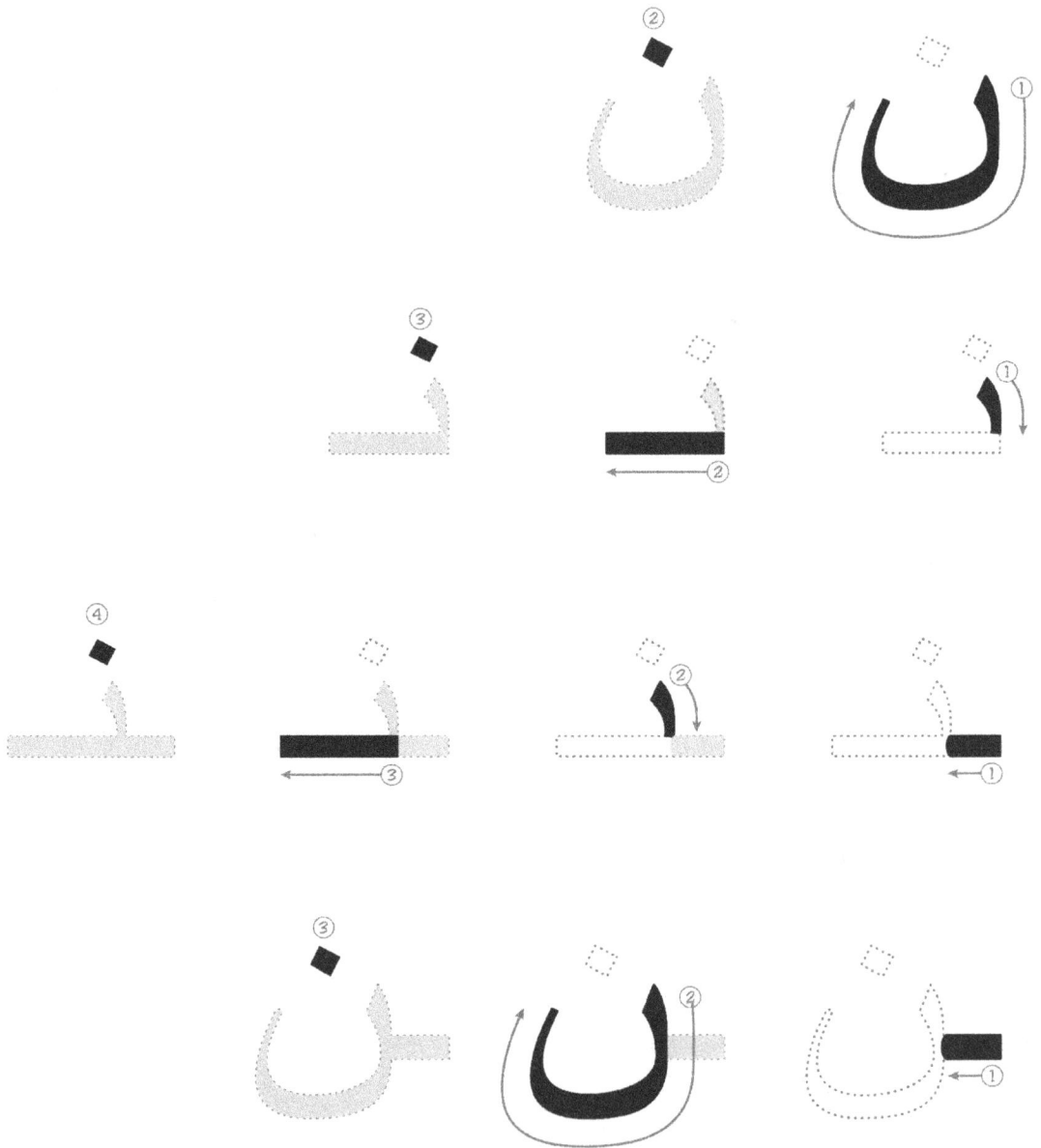

Writing Suggestions

ن   ﻨ   ﻧ

Stand-Alone Form
1. Stand-Alone Noon is a genie belly with a navel dot above it. Draw the belly as a big long stroke starting on the right. It is cup-shaped, like a fish-bowl--almost three sides of a square, but still rounded. This shape is just the same as the bowl at the end of Saad, or the handle of Seen.
2. The Navel is high, floating completely above the belly shape you just drew. Center it from left to right.

Beginning Form
1. Draw the finternails by starting above the line and coming down. This is the same familiar shape as Baa', taa', and thaa'.
2. Make a hard corner. Continue on the line to the left, on to the next letter.
3. Come back later on and add the dot over his nails.

Middle Form
1. you're coming in from the right.
2,3,4. Pick up your pen, jump a third of the way up, and draw a straight stroke down-wards. Continue on like the Beginning Form.

Ending Form
1. You're coming in from the right.
2. Pick up your pen, and go about a third of the way up. Draw a bowl shape, going down, around to the left, and then back up again. The left side of the bowl finishes at the same height that the right side of the bowl starts at. The bowl goes below the line about as much as it goes above the line.
3. At the single jewele for the Navel, centered above the bowl.

Writing Practice

Say the name of the letter, and make its sound,
each time you write the letter.

Writing Practice

Now put them together.
Remember to keep each letter
separate in your mind.

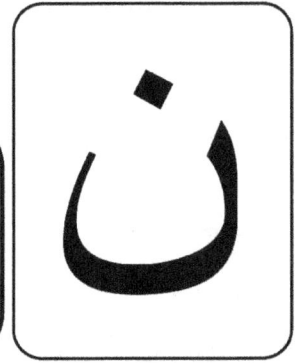

‫ـن‬	‫ـنـ‬	‫نـ‬	‫ن‬

Know The Difference!

Zaay is longer, and descends below the line. It is always unjoined on the left.

ز

Baa' has one dot, but it is on the BAAttom side of the line.

ب

taa' has TWO dots on TAAP. It's the Twins on the Toboggin.

ت

Daad the Dancing Dog on the Dune has a dot on top, but it's on top of the sand Dune. Even the ending form still has the dot on top of the Dune.

ض

dhaal is shaped like the oTHer SouTHern moTHer duck. It has a duck tail, and is not connected to the next letter on the left.

ذ

Khaa' is Khubla Khan Bach's Khap. It is khurved and does not point straight up.

خ

Reading Practice

مَن

n a m
man
who

مِن

n i m
min
from, of

نعم

m ª n
naªam
Yes

لكن

n k L
lakin
but

نار

r A n
naar
fire

صَنَعَ

a ª a n a S
Sanaªa
to make, to do

سينما

A m n y s
seenamaa
cinema

نحن

n H n
naHnu
we

haa'

h

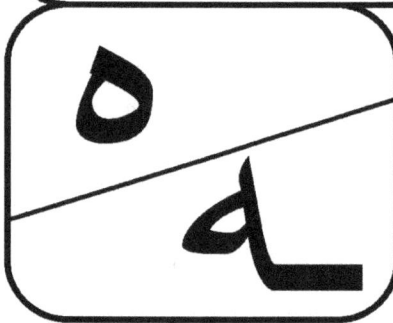

هاء

haa' sounds like the familiar (light) "h".
It comes from the front of the mouth.

h   *haa' CONNECTS on the left.*   h

haa'
is the Helpful Heroes

Heroic Henry
Helpful Hummingbird
and Happy Horse
watch over the tiny
Hummingbird Egg
all by itself--
    haa' haa' haa'!

Helpful Hints

haa' is one of the few letters to actually have four completely separate forms.

haa' also uses two different forms for ending words. If the previous letter wants to connect on the left, it uses the Happy Horse ending form. However, if the previous letter does _not_ want to connect on the left, it uses the Hummingbird Egg form, which is also the stand-alone form.

The taa'-maRbuuTah letter does this as well, as we'll see later on in this book.

Now You Sketch It--Doodles!

How To Write It

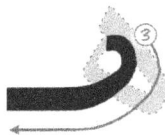

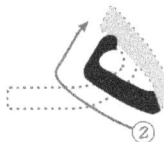

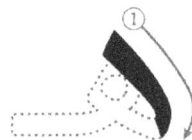

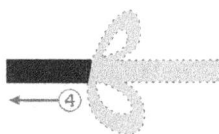

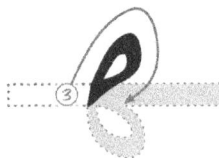

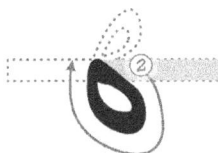

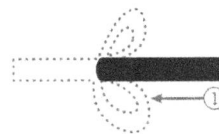

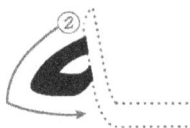

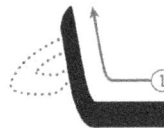

Writing Suggestions

Stand-Alone Form

1. The Humming-bird egg is very simple. It sits on top of the line. Simply start at the top, come down on the right side, and draw a complete loop. There is only ONE corner, at the top pointing upwards. The rest is round. The egg is about half the size of the line high, larger than a Meem.

Beginning Form

1. Start three-fourths of the way up, and draw the cape downwards. It's round.
2. Continue on smoothly and draw the hood. It's a loop that comes up and around.
3. Finish the loop of the hood, and continue on the line, on to the next letter.

Middle Form

1. You're coming in on the line from the previous letter on the right.
2. Make a hard, tight corner and draw the bottom wing. You have to draw the back, right-hand side of the loop for the wing before you draw the left, front side (go clockwise to start out). This is important.
3. Continue smoothly and finish the front of the top wing, then loop to draw the back of the top wing (keep going smoothly clockwise). This is important, too.
4. Continue on the line, connecting on to the next letter on the left.

Ending Form (Horsey version. Egg is same as Stand-Alone.)

1. You're coming in on the line. Make a corner and go upwards straight, on a diagonal. That's his neck. Leave room for his ear.
2. Lift your pen and drop down slightly. Make the horsey head starting from the top, with a tight loop that comes around, ending on the bottom. The horsey head top is below the top of his neck line, or else he won't have an ear. The head bottom ends up *above* the line, or else he won't have a neck. No giraffes, no wiener dogs.

Writing Practice

Say the name of the letter, and make its sound,
each time you write the letter.

Writing Practice

Now put them together.
Remember to keep each letter
separate in your mind.

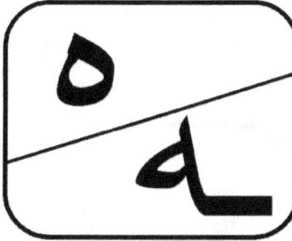

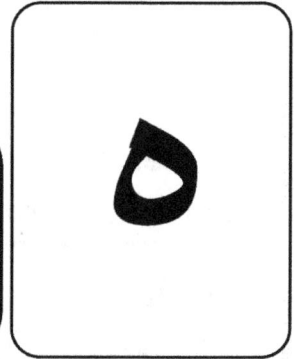

ه	ﻬ	ه	ه
ـه			

Know The Difference!

taa'-maRbuuTa looks like the horsey or the tiny hummingbird egg, except it only comes at the end of words and has a two-dot feminine crown over it.

ة ةـ

Ending ᵃayn and stand-alone ᵃayn loop backwards, like a singing lamb's ribbon or a shephard's crook.

ع عـ

Meem the Mini Mighty Mean Mung bean has a single loop at the beginning or middle, but a fancy tap root at the end.

مـ ـمـ ـم

Haa' is a completely different letter. It looks like Hot Harry's Hat, or a Hot Halapeno pepper.

حـ ح

Beginning ᵃayn is an open singing lamb's mouth. Middle ᵃayn is a lamb's ribbon; it has a single loop that is flat on top.

ـعـ عـ

Stand-alone Laam-Alif looks like a singing eeL from L.A. going "LA". It is not joined to the next letter on the left.

لا

Reading Practice

له

h L
lahu
his, he has ~

لها

A h L
lahaa
her

هي

y h
hiya
she, her

هو

w h
huwa
he, him

هذه

h dh h
hadhihi
this [feminine]

هم

m h
hum
they

فواكه

h k A w f
fawaakih
fruit

هاتف

f t A h
haatif
phone

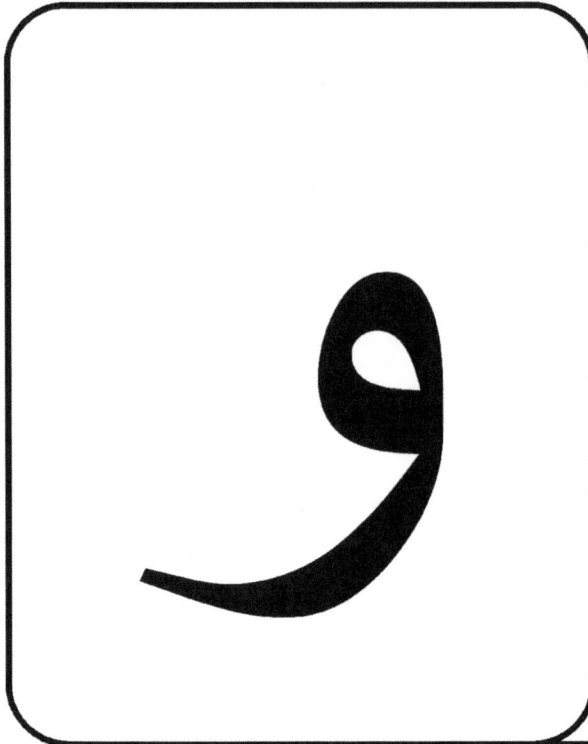

WOW

W
uu

و

و ـ | ـ و ـ | ـ و

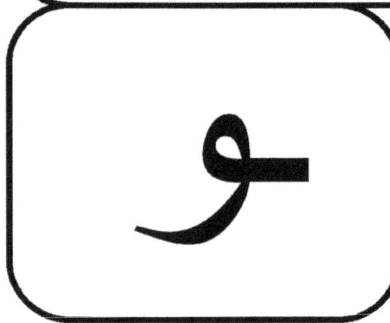

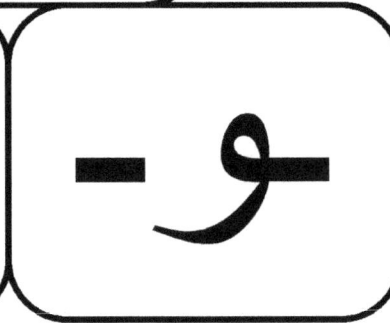

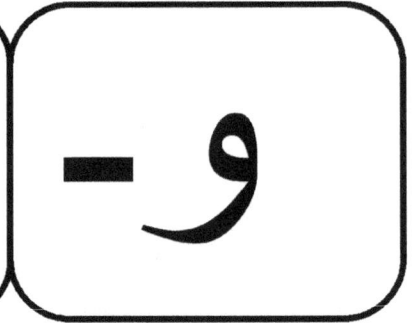

☾★ *"bilabial approximant / long high back vowel"* واو

Wow, like the English letter "y", actually has two pronunciations. It can be used as a consonant, like the
familiar "w" in "want". Or, it can be used as a long
vowel, like the familiar "oo" sound in "two" or "stew".

w / oo   *Wow DOES NOT connect on the left.*   w, uu/oo/ū

74

WOW

is the Wow Wide Towel roll

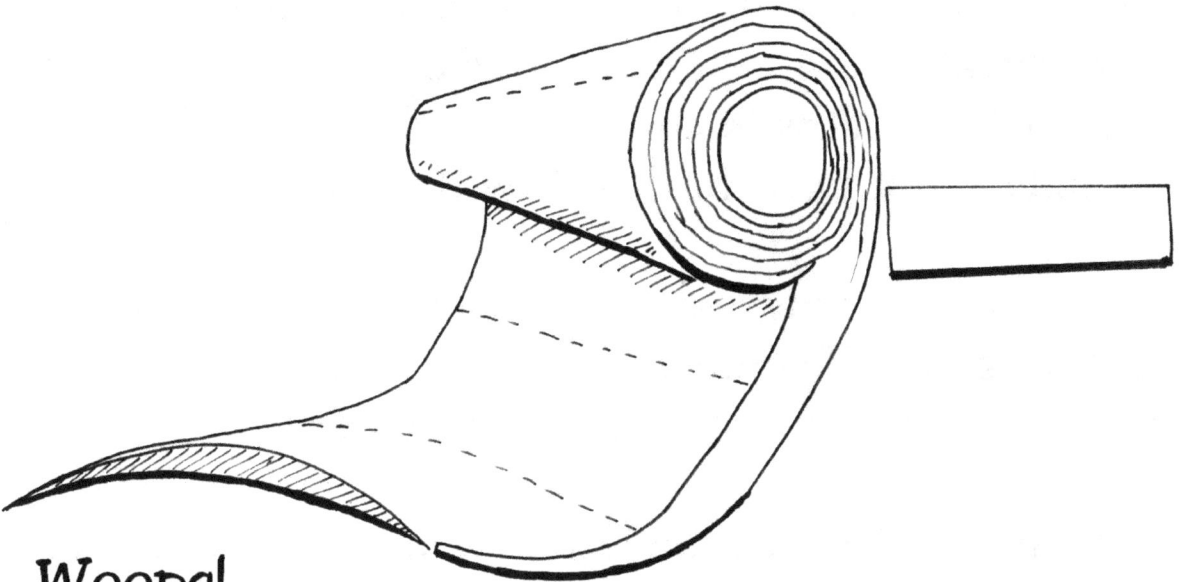

Woops!
Double You and You will Want to Watch
this useful spool of Wow Wide Paper Towel
Wisely used to wash and wipe up
food, stew, fuel,
and wet warm water.
Wow!

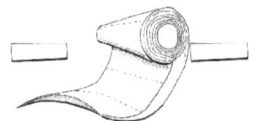

Helpful Hints

Wow is the second long vowel letter out of three, in the set 'aalif, wow, and yaa'. It can be used as either a consonant or a vowel. When used as a consonant, it has the "w" sound of "wipe". And when used as a long vowel, it has the "uu" sound of "food", sometimes spelled "oo". Wow is not connected on the left, and it extends about two-thirds below the line.

Wow is a long vowel and a true letter. It is the long "uu" version of Damma, the short vowel "u", which is not a true letter but only a diacritic mark.

The name of our English letter "double-U" shows that historically it was first written "uu". So w and uu are the same. This will help you to remember which letter to use.

Wow is the second-most common letter in the Arabic dictionary, being present in 18% of all words.

Now You Sketch It--Doodles!

How To Write It

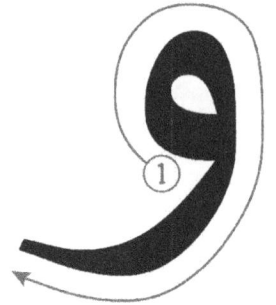

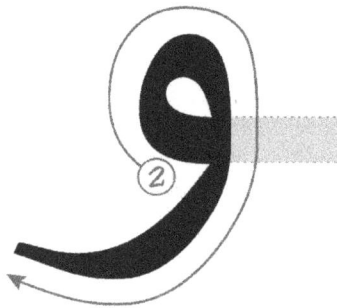

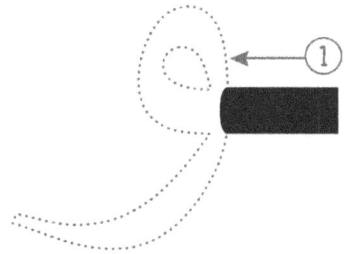

Writing Suggestions

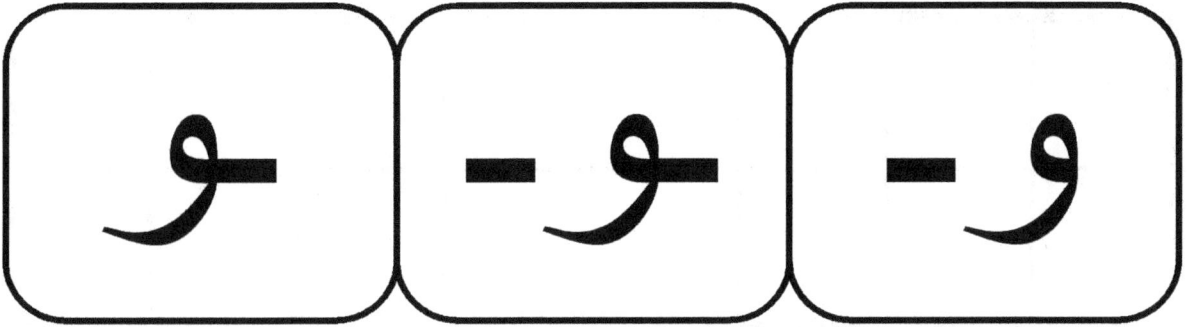

و - و - و

Stand-Alone Form

1. Start on the line. Go flat, sideways. Then make a rounded corner and go up, in a clockwise direction. Bring the rounded loop up, about one-fourth of the height above the line. Round the corner at the top. Then, start to make a sweeping curve that goes from one-fourth above the line, down to cross the line and the previous start of the stroke, down two-thirds below the line, and then curling sideways. The stroke ends up below the line, just like a Roh'.

Beginning Form

Same as the Stand-Alone form. Wow is always unconnected, so leave a small space and start the next letter over with a Beginning form (unless the next letter is on the end, in which case it needs a Stand-Alone form).

Middle Form

1. You're coming in on the line from the previous connected letter.
2. Without picking your pen up, continue on a loop around clockwise one-fourth of the way up. Then draw a sweeping curve. Wow is unconnected, so the next letter needs to start over from the Beginning. Leave a short space until the next letter, here represented by a dash.

Ending Form

Same as the Middle Form.

Writing Practice

Say the name of the letter, and make its sound,
each time you write the letter.

Writing Practice

Here we cheat and use dashes
to represent other letters in the middle.
Use your own vocabulary words
if you wish.

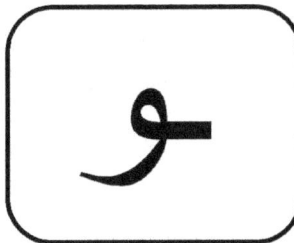

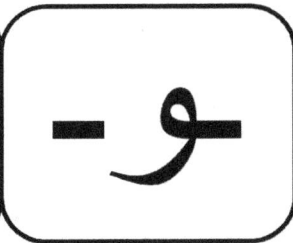

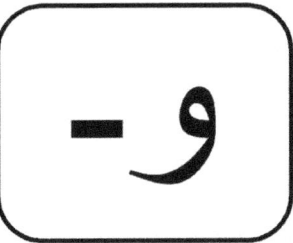

و	و -	- و	و

Know The Difference!

Fat Freddy Faa' has a dot over it. Faa' stands above the line. Its stand-alone or final form has a long Far, Far Flying Carpet.

 فـ فـ

Raa' has no loop. It looks like a Rowing oaR.

ر

Damma is a mark that is actually a tiny Wow, used to indicate a shorter U sound. It floats above a consonant, not in line, and is not an official letter.

ُو

Qaaf has a big, long tail which looks like a queen beckoning. Qaaf has a queen's crown of two dots.

ق

Meem the Mighty Mean Mung bean has a tap root that comes out of the left side and grows downwards.

مـ م

Final ᵃayn looks like a sitting lamb's ribbon that loops backwards, to the right.

ـع

Reading Practice

أو

w 'A
aw
or

و

w
wa
and; while; with; by

لهو

w h L
lahw
fun

ذو

w dh
dhuu
posessing, posessor of ~

واضح

H D A w
waaDiH
clear, obvious

ورق

q r w
waraq
paper

أموال

L A w m 'A
amwaal
funds

وحل

L H w
waHl
mud

yaa'

ي

y
ee

ى

ي

ـيـ

ـي

"palatial glide / long high front vowel"

ياء

Just like Y in English, Yaa' has two pronunciations.
It can be a consonant like the y in "you".
Or it can be a long vowel, like the y in "happy".
In the first case, it's normally written as "y".
In the second case, it's often written as "ii" or "ee".

i/y   *Yaa' CONNECTS on the left.*   y, ii/ee/ī

yaa'

is Yaah-Yaah Yippee Snakes on Skates

Easy Yippee roller skates
Yes they're fun for yelling snakes!
Year-old yellow young skates please me
Happy, Funny, it's so Ee-sy

Hee hee hee
Yippee! Yippee!
Yaah-Yaah snakes on skates for me!

Helpful Hints

Yaa' is the third long vowel in the Arabic alphabet, after 'Aalif and Wow. It's the last fully official letter in the Arabic alphabet.

Like Wow, Yaa' can be a consonant ("y") or a long vowel ("ii" or "ee"). It is the long counterpart to the short vowel Kasra ("i").

The full stand-alone version of Yaa' is our famous picture of "Snakes On Skates". In the fast beginning form, there is not enough space to draw the snake, so you just draw a picture of the roller-skate. This goes for the middle form as well.

When a hamza (which we'll finally be covering next) is riding a yaa', the snake loses its skates. This has the chance of being confused with an 'aalif-maqSura (which we'll also look at later in this book). Just remember that that clever little hamza takes the skates, but it's still a Yaa'.

Now You Sketch It--Doodles!

How To Write It

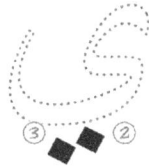

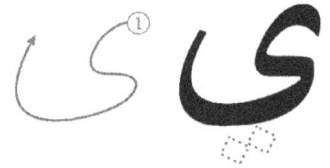

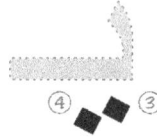

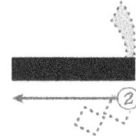

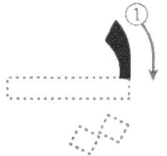

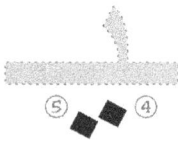

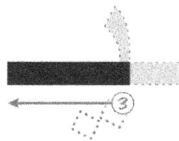

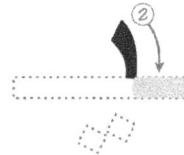

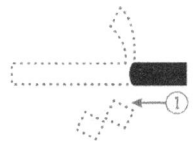

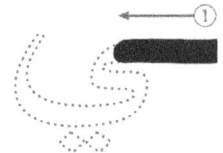

Writing Suggestions

ي   ـيـ   ـي

Stand-Alone Form

1. The Stand-Alone Form of the Yaah-Yaah Snakes on Skates is large and very fancy. It starts halfway above the line. There is a thick hook for the snake's head. The stroke arches counter-clockwise for the snake's neck. Then it has a rounded corner and goes flat on the line left to right. There is another rounded corner, and the snake's belly curves down in a slanted stroke to halfway under the line. It looks like the snake is driving up a ramp. The belly of the snake is slightly more than twice as long (wide) as the previous flat body of the snake. The back end of the snake forms the left half of a traditional bowl shape, and the snake's tail curves up to end up slightly above the line. The whole curve is elegant and balanced. It takes a bit of practicing to get this right, but it's worth it.

2. The two dots for the skates come centered under the snake's belly.. Remember, he's riding on these roller skates, so not too far away.

Beginning Form

No room for the snake here, we're just going to draw his roller skate.

1. Start one-third of the way up, just like a Beginning taa', thaa', or noon. Draw a slightly curving line down to the line.

2. Make a hard right-angle corner. Continue on the line, on to the next letter.

3. Sometime later, come back and put two dots under the corner. Slightly tilted.

Middle Form

The middle form is the same as the beginning form. Pick your pen up to draw stroke #2.

Ending Form

The Ending Form is a much flatter version of the Stand-Alone Form. It is all under the line, except for the tip of the snake's tail.

1. You're coming in on the line, from the previous connected letter.

2. Without picking your pen up, draw a curving snake swoosh. This time, the snake's belly is flat, not driving up-hill. And his tail ends up just barely above the line.

3. Finish with the two skate wheel dots, centered. This time they are flat, not tilted.

Writing Practice

Say the name of the letter, and make its sound,
each time you write the letter.

Writing Practice

Now put them together.
Remember to keep each letter
separate in your mind.

ـي	ـيـ	يـ	ي

Know The Difference!

Aalif MaQSuura, the Aalif in the shape of a Yaa', is a snake relaxing without her roller skates in a hot pool, going "Aah".

ى

noon has a single dot, the Nice Norman geNie's Navel, above it.

ن

Sod the Sad, Sod Sand dune has a dune with a hill-crest to the right of a deep pool.

ص

baa' only has a single Ball-Bearing BB dot on the BAAttom.

ب

taa' has two dots but they are on TAAp of the Toboggin.

ت

seen has the Silly Spectacles right beside the handle.

س

Reading Practice

أي

y 'A
ayy
which

أين

a n y 'A
ayna
where

بيت

t y b
bayt
house

دين

n y d
deen
religion

فيلم

m L y f
fylm
movie

كرسي

y s r k
kursee
chair

صديق

q y d S
Sadeeq
friend

طيب

b y T
Tayyib
O.K.

Bonus Marks

Congratulations! Yaa' marks the end of what most people consider to be the "official" alphabet.

However, some people consider hamza to be an official letter and therefore the last letter. So you're about to learn this next.

English has abbreviations like &, @, and # that are not "official" letters, but are used all the time and everyone understands what they mean anyway. They're kind of irregular.

Just the same, Arabic has a number of important abbreviations that do not belong to the "official" alphabet, but none-the-less are needed for a full coverage. We're going to hit the five main ones for you.

This will give you a full introduction to all of the major letters used to make words in Arabic.

hamza

,

ع

ء

ـــــــــ

أ

"glottal stop"

هَمْزة

Hamza has a unique sound. It is the sound of silence! But it is a special kind of silence made by keeping your throat and mouth perfectly still, just for a quarter of a second. Your throat freezes in place, really fast. So the sound stops all of a sudden, and then starts up again all of a sudden.

English has this sound in the middle of the word "Uh-Oh".

2

'/-/#

hamza

is the hiccupping surfing hamster

Uh-oh!
It's the hiccupping hamster
hamza
on his up-ended, slick-trick
go-anywhere surfboard!
Hold your breath as he does his thing!
Total silence...

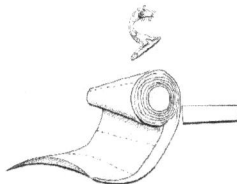

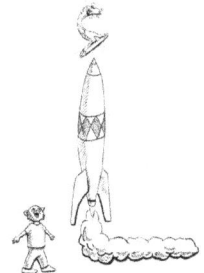

Helpful Hints

If you just say the first half of "Uh-Oh"--- "Uh-" ---you'll notice that the hamza sound can easily come at the end of words. And then, if you just say the second half-- "-Oh" -- you'll be able to see that the hamza can even <u>start</u> words. You keep your throat still, then start all of a sudden.

Cockney English uses this sound a lot, especially to replace "H" at the beginning of words. In the musical "My Fair Lady", Eliza Dolittle sings "Oll Oi won' is 'Enry 'Iggins 'ead!".

The hamza is a crazy letter. Normally it occurs as a mark--it has to balance on top of another carrier letter that it rides, like a hamster surfing a wave. It can appear on top of any of the long vowel letters: 'aalif, wow, or yaa', in any of their forms. It can even appear on top of the left side of a laam-'aalif! Sometimes it appears <u>underneath</u> an 'aalif, when it's used with a kasra. And when it shows up all by itself at the end of a word, it is written full-sized, like any other letter.

hamza is never connected.

When hamza rides on a yaa', the yaa' loses both its dots.
Remember: **The hamster takes the skates of snakes!**

Technically, an 'aalif at the beginning of a word should always have a hamza on it, since words aren't supposed to start with vowels. The silence of a hamza is considered to be a <u>consonant</u>, and therefore this gets around this requirement. But since it's forced, Modern Arabic will often leave the hamza out when writing a hamza on top of an alif at the beginning of words. Hamzas in the middle and at the end should always be written.

Hamza is not considered to be an "official" letter by most people. It may occur alphabetically at the end, after the yaa'; or it could come at the beginning, mixed in with the 'aalif.

Again, some people say that hamza is the last letter of the alphabet, after yaa'. Most people say hamza is a separate letter, like "@" in English, that is not a "real letter". Then yaa' is the last letter of the official alphabet. And because hamza has to ride an 'Aalif to start out, in this case hamza is actually listed alphabetically mixed in with 'Aalif as an irregular exception, and before baa'.

Remember, although hamza is a silence, technically it counts as a consonant. It is often put at the beginning of words that look like they start with a vowel, so that they can be said to start with a consonant. It's a convention.

Now You Sketch It--Doodles!

How To Write It

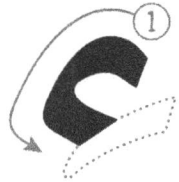

Writing Suggestions

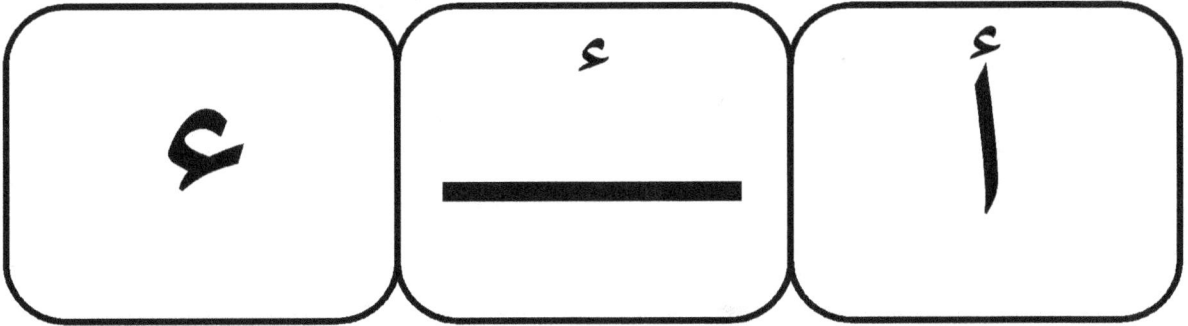

ء ____ أ

Stand-Alone and Ending Forms

Stand-alone or Ending hamza is a medium-small letter, one-third of a full height tall, about the size of a meem mung bean loop or a haa' humming-bird egg. It sits on top of the line, like an English letter "c". First, draw the surfing hamster shape, starting on the upper right and coming around to the lower left. Then, pick your pen up, and draw the surfboard that the hamster is standing on. In this case, it's a bold, diagonal, slightly curving stroke that begins slightly in front of the hamster's nose, and ends just under his tail. For the larger Stand-alone or Ending forms, the surfboard is emphasized and the hamster is standing on the *back* of the board. But for the faster, smaller *accent* signs, the strokes all flow together and the hamster stands on the *front* of the board, "hanging ten". The hamza is always unconnected.

Beginning and Middle Forms

Beginning or Middle hamza is a *tiny* mark, about the same size as a fatHa-tein or a kasRa-tein. Like both of these, it needs to ride on top of or underneath another letter, preferrably one of the long vowels. Don't pick your pen up when drawing the tiny version. Make sure the surfboard part is flat, and on the diagonal.

Writing Practice

Say the name of the letter, and make its sound,
each time you write the letter.

Writing Practice

Now put them together.
Remember to keep each letter
separate in your mind.

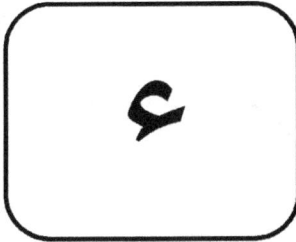

ع	ـ	أ	ع

Know The Difference!

Fat-Ha is only a single stroke, without the surfing hiccuping Hamster.
It only appears above the line.

ﹷ

Kasra is only a single stroke.
It only appears below the line.

ﹻ

Beginning ªayn is flat on the bottom. It is connected on the left to the next letter, and is normal-sized when compared to the letters around it.

ع

Dom-mah, the New Blue Loop of Wool from the Spool, is shaped like a tiny Wow and sounds like U.

ُ

Dom-matein, the Ruined Spoon of Brigadoon, only comes at the end of a word. It's a Dom-mah ending in N.
It looks like a bent spoon.

ٌ

Kaaf has a bucKle inside its sKi boot. This is part of the letter. (Whoever heard of a ski boot without buckles?)

كا

Reading Practice

أين

n y ʻa
ayna
where

ماء

ʻ A m
maa'
water

غداء

ʻ A d gh
ghadaa'
lunch

مائي

y ʻ A m
maa'y
aquatic

لؤلؤ

ʻw L ʻw L
luu'luu'
pearls

رأس

s ʻA r
raa's
head

إبن

n b A ʻ
ibn
son

قارئ

ʻy r A q
qaaree'
reader

taa' marbuuTah

a

ة

"feminine marker--short low back vowel"

تاء مَربوطة

taa' marbuuTah only comes at the end of a word.

It makes the word feminine.

It's normally pronounced "ah", with a short "a" like "father".

(However, when it's followed by a possessive ending, which has a vowel,

the taa' marbuuTah changes back into a "t" sound

so you won't have two vowels in a row.)

a/h

a / ah

taa' marbuuTah

is the Crowned "T" Marble in Utah

Ah! How feminine!
Tha' Marble-Utah!
Two dots crowning an egg or a horse
Let you know the "ah" ending
Is feminine, of course.

Helpful Hints

You can remember taa' marbuutTah by thinking of a big marble ball that comes from Utah. It has a big "T" coming out of the top--that's where the two points come from.

taa' marbuuTah, the "silent t", is a different way to write taa' when it's not pronounced. It symbolizes a grammatical ending for feminine words.

Although the current crowned hummingbird-egg looks a lot like the letter haa', historically the taa' marbuuTah used to be a form of the letter taa'. The current taa' has an open dish or toboggin with two points above it. And the taa' marbuuTah has a closed circle with the toboggin curled up into an egg, with the same two points above. That's why you'll often see taa' marbuuTah coming between "taa'" listings in the dictionary.

Just like with haa', the horsey form comes after letters that want to connect on the left, and the hummingbird-egg form comes after letters that don't want to connect on the left.
taa' marbuuTah **only** appears at the **end** of a word.

Technically, all feminine words that end in taa' marbuuTah also have an invisible fatHa before the taa-marbuuTah as part of the feminine ending. This fatHa normally isn't written, however. But that's where the "a" sound comes from. Technically.

In certain grammar situations, the taa' marbuuTah will actually change back into a regular taa'. This happens when you add word endings onto the end. Don't worry about it until you have to.

Now You Sketch It--Doodles!

How To Write It

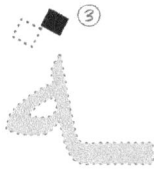

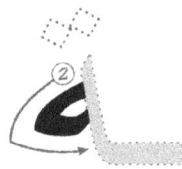

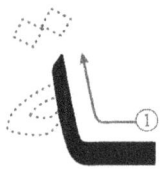

Writing Suggestions

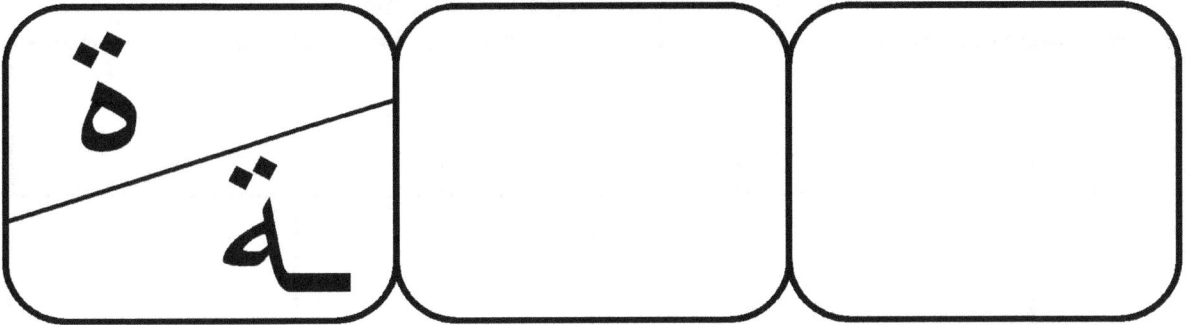

Stand-Alone Form

taa' marbuuTah, the "silent t" that looks like a haa', only comes at the end of words. But when you talk about the letter itself, it's drawn like a haa' hummingbird egg with two dots crowning it, just like the two tots on the toboggan. First, draw the hummingbird egg with a clockwise circle starting at the top; it sits on top of the line. It has one corner pointing straight up. Next, put the two dots right over the top of the egg.

Beginning and Middle Forms

taa' marbuuTah does not have a beginning nor a middle form. It only appears at the end of a word.

Ending Form

Just like haa', there are two ending forms, depending on if the previous letter is unconnected or connected. The unconnected version is the same as the stand-alone form--the hummingbird egg with two dots over it. The connected version looks like a horsey with two dots over its head. First, continuing on from the previous letter, draw the body and the neck of the horsey. Then draw its head, remembering to leave a short ear at the top. Put one dot right above the ear, and the other next to it above the head.

Writing Practice

Say the name of the letter, and make its sound,
each time you write the letter.

Writing Practice

This letter only comes at the end of words.
Use the vocabulary in
"Reading Practice"
to write down words in the spaces.

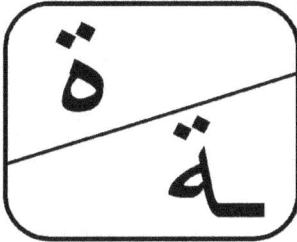

ة / ﺔ			ة

Know The Difference!

haa' has no dots on its Humming-bird egg.	ه
haa' has no crown on its Horsey.	ـه
Middle Qaaf is connected, and has a stem on its loop. Ending Qaaf has a beckoning hand to the left.	ق ـق
Meem the Mighty Mean Mung bean has no dots over it. Final Meem always has a root following it.	مـمـم مـ
taa' can come at the beginning or middle of words, as well as the end. It has the Toboggin with the Twin dots on TAAp.	ـتـ ت تـ
Yaa' has two dots on the bottom, for the Yippee snakes on roller skates.	يـ ي

114

Reading Practice

زوجة

a j w z
zawja
wife

تلة

a L t
talla
hill

حفرة

a r f H
Hufra
hole

بيرة

a r y b
beera
beer

قهوة

a w h q
qahwa
coffee

طاقة

a q A T
Taaqa
energy

laa

لا ـلا ـلا

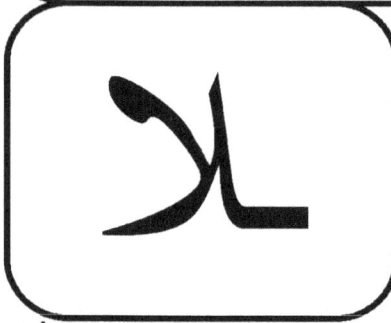

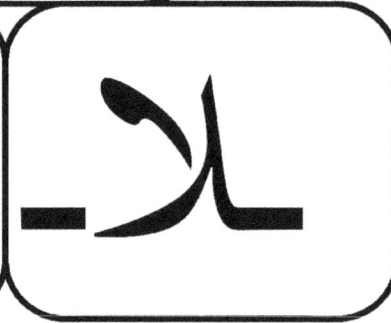

"alveolar lateral with long low back vowel"

لام أَلِف

Laam-'aalif is simply an L put together with a long A.
So it always sounds like "Laah".

la   *Laam-'aalif DOES NOT connect on the left.*   laa/lā

laam-'aalif

is the Singing Eel from L.A.

LA

LA

LA

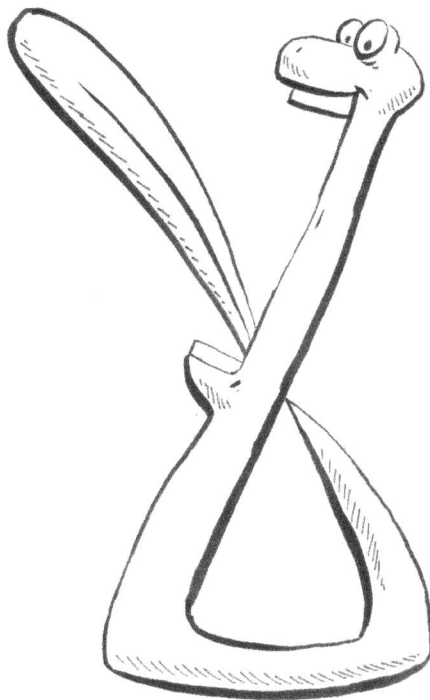

"LA LA LA..."
He wants to be a star!
The Singing Eel will make you feel
As happy as you are!
With an "L" and an "A" and an "L - A LA"
It's easy now to see
Just dance and sing like anything
And you'll "LA LA" like me!!

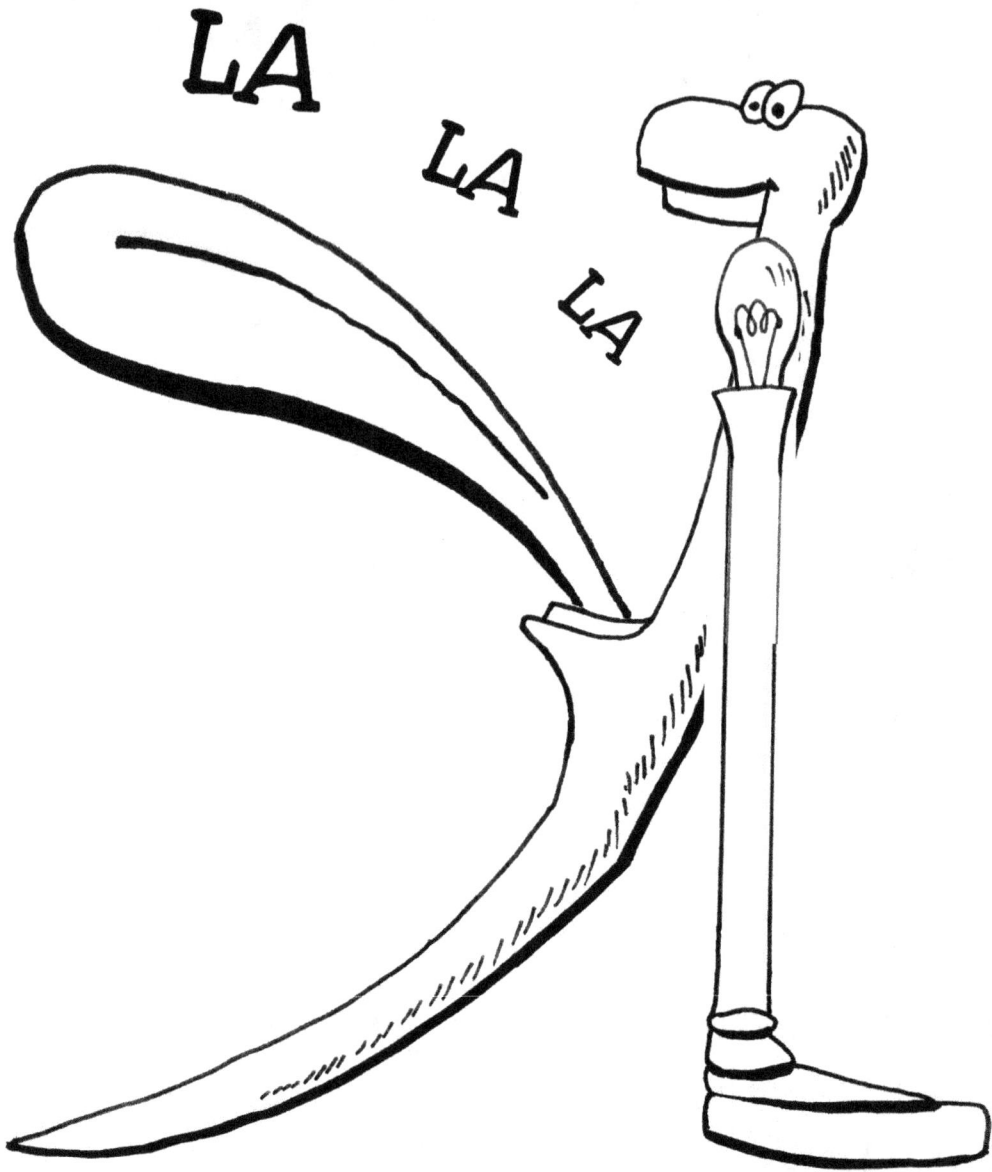

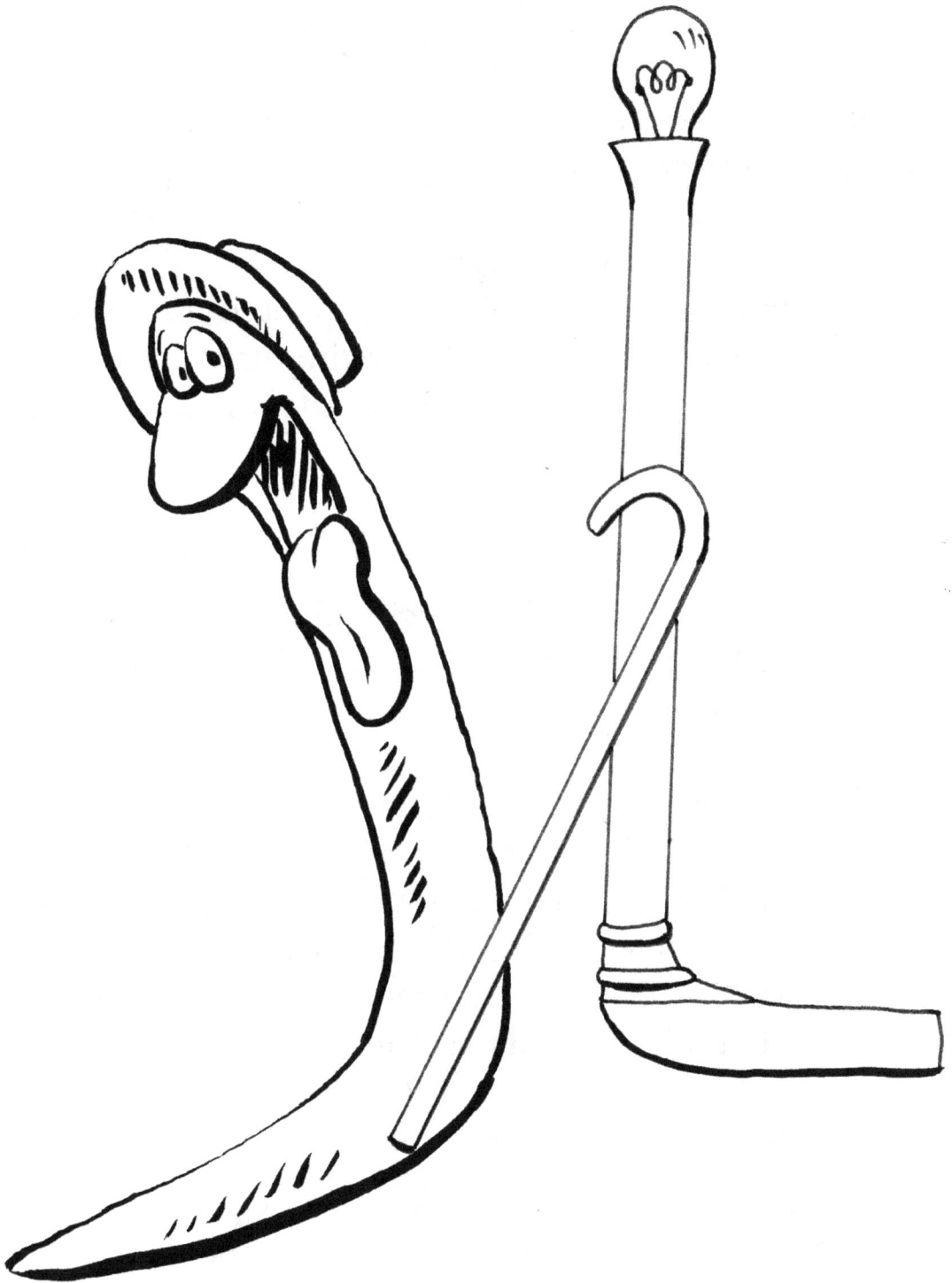

Helpful Hints

The singing electric eel from L.A. has two different ending forms, depending upon the type-font. Some people like to draw the eel high up, leaning on his favorite lamp-post. Then the tongue can be separate from the eel. Whereas, some people like to draw the lamp-post, then draw the eel separately, then draw a small dancing-cane between them afterwards. This puts the eel lower down. Either way, it's a good way to write LA.

Laam-'Aalif came about because if you put L ل together with A ا normally, لا , it just looks weird.
So they had to come up with some abbreviation to make it look different.

The fact that this is an abbreviation, like using "Mr." for "mister", can be seen when you look at how this combines. Remember that 'Aalif can be drawn as a seat for hamza on the top (to indicate fatHa), or a hamza on the bottom (to indicate kasRa). But the 'Aalif is not pronounced in this case. Well, the LA inherits this feature.

Laam fatHa (la, NOT laa) is ﻷ or ﻷ ,

whereas Laam kasRa (li) is ﻹ or ﻹ !

Now You Sketch It--Doodles!

How To Write It

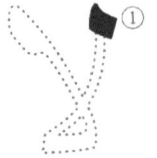

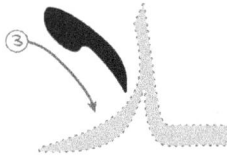

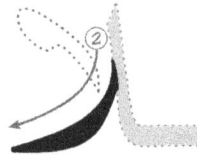

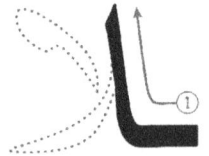

Writing Suggestions

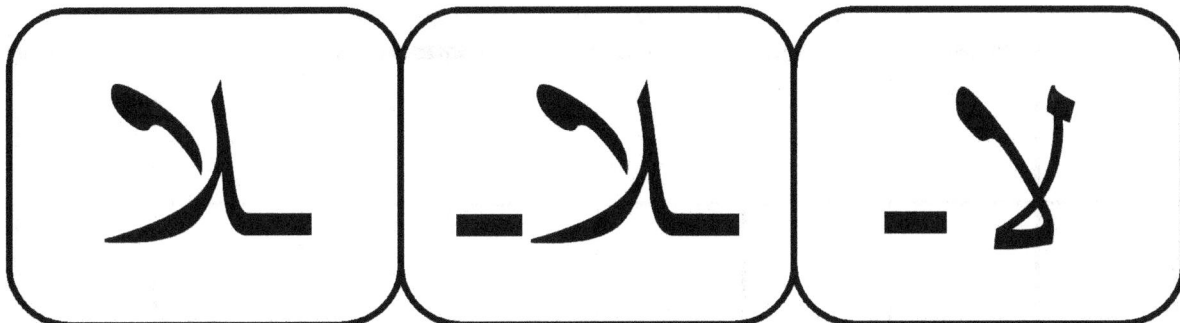

Stand-Alone and Beginning Forms

LA would normally go straight down to the line, have a small horizontal segment that goes across right-to-left, and then go straight up. But that makes too many straight lines together in one place, it makes it too hard to read. So, the LA abbreviation switches which side the bottom parts come down on, to make a loop at the bottom and to make things easier to see.

1. Make a small tic mark (or "serif") up at the top, as if starting a normal Laam.
2. Start coming down straight, but then change your mind and curve down to the left corner. This is the eel from L.A.'s open mouth.
3. Make a hard corner. Come back left-to-right down at the bottom, flat. This is the eel's stomach, mostly flat on the ground. The back end comes back to almost under his head.
4. Arch outwards, all the way up to the top, to where the end of the 'Aalif _should_ be if you were drawing it straight. That's the eel's tongue. Put a big blob on the end, so it's obvious. Make sure the top of the tongue is as tall as the eel's head.

Middle and Ending Forms

1. Come in from the previous letter on the line. Take a rounded corner, and go straight up. This is the lamp-post. It is full height, as high as a normal Laam, but with no mark on top.
2. Come down in a curving sweep, but this time go out far. Ending Laam-'Aalif is a wide, fancy letter. This is the eel's tail, leaning against the lamp-post.
3. Pick up your pen and start on the outsite, high up, above the tail and beside the lamp-post top. Draw a blob, and then a curving swish inwards. That's his tongue.

--It seems that some people draw the #3 stroke, the entire dancing eel, second. And then they come back to connect the lamp-post to the eel with a little dancing cane stroke. This is not approved, but you should be able to recognize it when you see it.

Writing Practice

Say the name of the letter, and make its sound,
each time you write the letter.

Writing Practice

Now put them together.
Remember to keep each letter
separate in your mind.

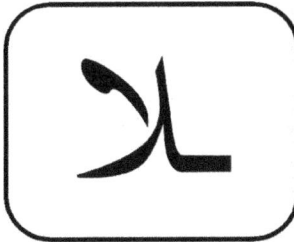

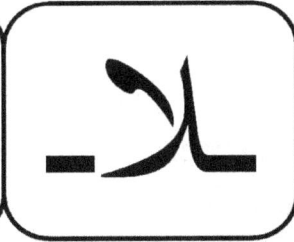

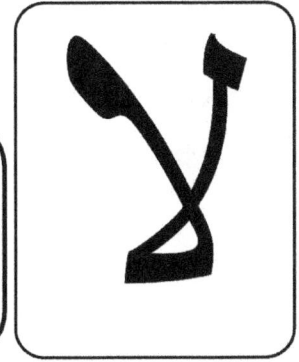

لا	لا	لا	لا

Know The Difference!

Kaaf looks like Kris Kringle sKiing, or his sKi boot. Kaaf is big and angular. The sKi boot has bucKles.

كـ كـ ك

Laam by itself, without the following Aalif, looks like a Lamp post or a Leaning backwards eeL. It is a very simple letter.

لـ لـ ل

'Aalif by itself, or after another letter, is even more simple.

ا لـ ا

haa' has Heroic Henry's cape, or Helpful Hummingbird. They are connected to the next letter on the left.

هـ هـ

Final ªein has a loop and a sitting lamb's ribbon that curls downward below the line.

عـ

Taa' the Tall, Tall Tower has a hill right next to it.

ط

Reading Practice

لاأحد

d H 'A LA
laa'aHad
nobody

لا

LA
laa
not ~ing, no (verb)

الأحد

d H L'A A
aal'aaHad
Sunday

لايهمّ

2 m h y LA
laayahumm
Never mind!

سلام

m LA s
salaam
Peace

خلاّب

b 2LA kh
khallaab
pretty (place, thing)

أهلاًوسهلاً

an LA h s w an LA h 'A
ahlan wa sahlan
Welcome, welcome!

الإبن

n b LA' A
al-'ibn
the son

Special Note

It would not be possible to cover Arabic culture without looking at the most important word in the Arabic language.

الله   or   أَللّٰه

h 2L L a
al-Laah
God

You would think, with a Laam followed by an 'Aalif like this, that the word Allah would have a Laam-'Aalif character in it. But no.

This is an extremely old word--so old, it is said, that the spelling got fixed in place before there were any 'Aalifs in the written language. You will notice that the second 'Aalif between the Laam and the haa' is completely missing. It's the traditional way of spelling it like that. Instead, there is a "pronunciation mark" of a tiny 'Aalif above the shad-dah, called a "dagger 'Aalif", so that people will remember to put the long 'Aalif back in when they say "Allaah".

"al" means "the", you will remember, and the common word for "god" is "ilaah". So "al-Laah" actually is closer to "The Deity". It's more of a title, and not so much a name.

The second L is pronounced as a special ringing, dark L from the back of the throat (like "bottle"). Maybe that's why it has the shad-dah over it. It's special, different from the light L Laam normally used in Arabic.

The letters are often extremely stylized, and can be quite hard to read. However, the A-L-L three-lines combination is pretty hard to miss. Because this word is so stylized and so important, the entire word, all together, is given its own character (letter) in the computer Unicode alphabet: U+FDF2. ﷲ

The fact that "Allaah" in Arabic translates into "God" in English is shown by the fact that both Arab Jews and Christians also use "Allaah" to talk about God. In fact, Arab Christians use three terms: "Allaah al-'ab" (God the Father), "Allaah al-ibn" (God the Son), and "Allaah al-RuuH al-Quds" (God the Holy Spirit). So the word "Allaah" in Arabic simply means the same that the word "God" means in English.

Some silly people have used this naming difference as an excuse to start fights. You do not see people complaining as if they own the Moon, and so if other people call it "al Qamar" they must be talking about something completely different--as if the Moon were different on the other side of the earth. And yet a number of people--on all sides--have been talking as if they own The Deity. This has caused problems.

People fear that which they do not understand. And people all over the world want to band together into cultures. Then they are tempted to show contempt to other cultures as an easy way to look big. But good people are good all over the world. When people have the courage to step outside and learn different cultures, then there is understanding--and then there is no need to fear. When good people can get together and handle problems across cultures, then--we believe--that's when you start to get real peace. We hope this course helps you with what you want to achieve in your life.

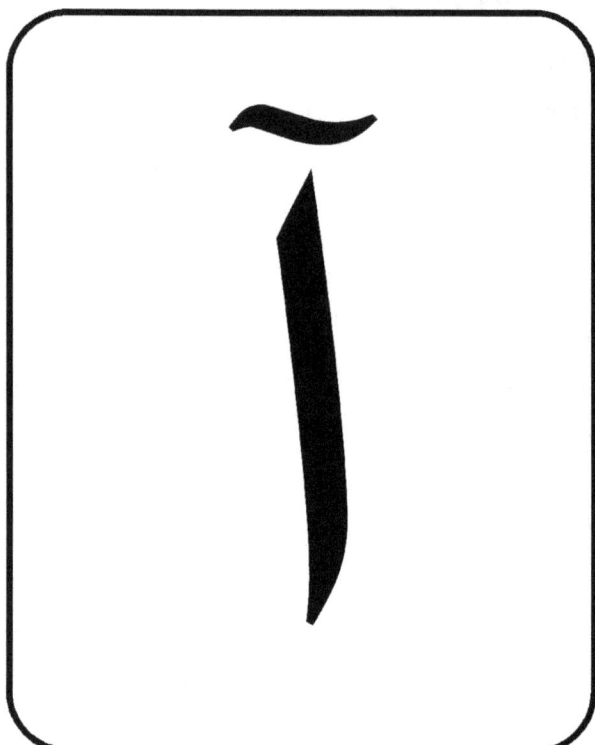

'aa

‘aa

ٱ ‌ـٰ ‌ـٰٓ

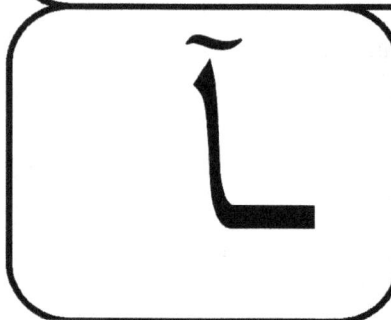

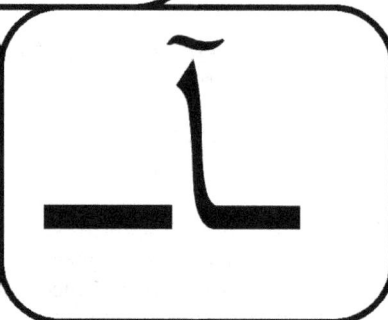

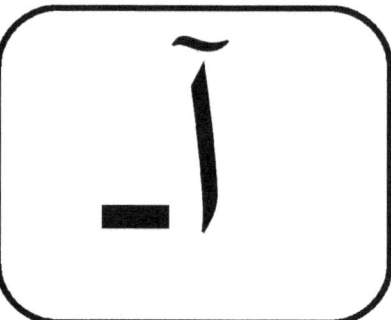

☪ *glottal stop with long low back vowel"* أَلِف مَدَّ

'Aalif-mad-da is a contraction for a hamza over an
'aalif followed immediately by *another* long 'aalif.
It is pronounced like a hamza pause followed by an
especially long 'aalif: "-'-aaah".

a   'Aalif-mad-da DOES NOT connect on the left.   'aa/'ā

130

'aalif mad-da

is the Rocket with the Potato Chip

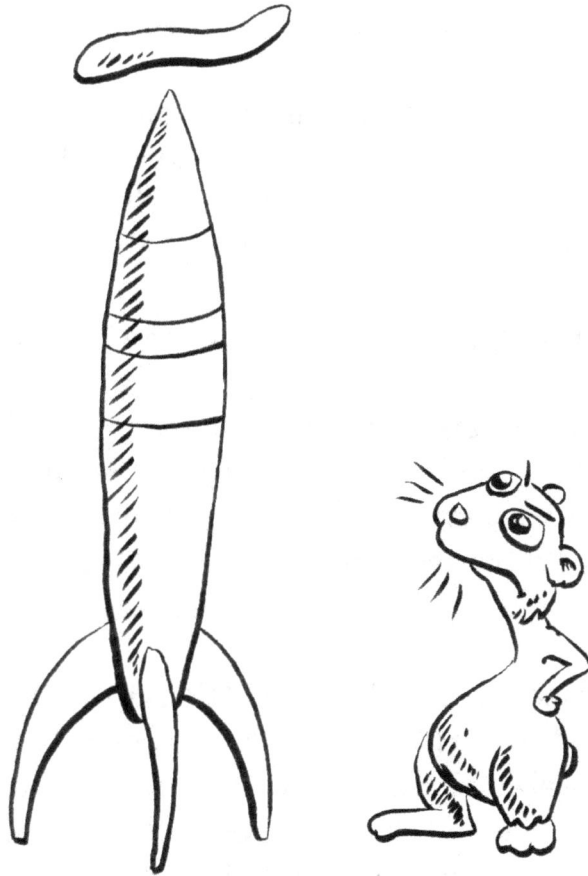

A potato-chip balanced on tall rocket tip
Is titled as 'Aalif Mad-da.
The hamsta' is saying that _he_ should be first--
But that would take too much to draw.

Helpful Hints

'Aalif mad-da is also technically a contraction for *two* hamzas put together. Two hamzas in a row are almost impossible to say. They get replaced with a hamza (riding an 'Aalif) followed by a long 'Aalif. But then that gets replaced by the 'Aalif mad-da.

It would be real ugly to write down two hamzas next to each other. And it would still be ugly to write down a hamza riding an 'Aalif followed immediately by another 'Aalif, it's just too many lines together. So that's why this contraction came about.

Although it's supposed to be about the hamza, the hamza disappears!

And so that's where our picture comes from. Look how upset he is! The hamster is madder because *he* wanted to be the one riding his surf-board up on top of the rocket. But he doesn't even get to appear in this letter. No hamsta', even though he is supposed to be there! And that's a good way to remember why it's called **madda**.

The 'Aalif mad-da tilde looks a little bit like a fatHa, but not much. And it's always drawn riding directly on top of the 'Aalif. No hamza to be found. In Arabic, there is only this one symbol that has a tilde in it, and it always comes on top of an 'Aalif. You don't have to worry about it coming on the bottom, or around anything else except the 'Aalif.

(Note however that when an 'Aalif gets abbreviated as part of an L.A., then the tilde still rides the 'Aalif. Except the 'Aalif has been turned into the eel's tongue. So you've got a potato-chip sitting on top of a tongue, which reminds you to say the "aaah" extra long.)

Now You Sketch It--Doodles!

How To Write It

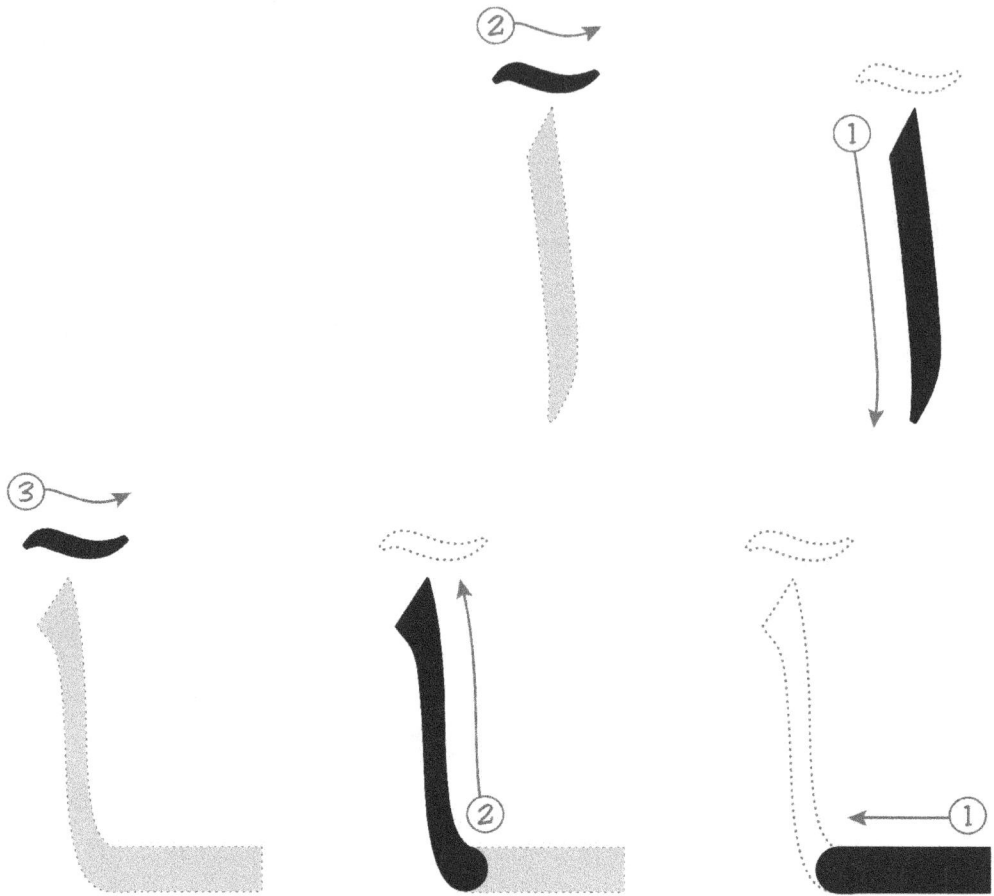

Writing Suggestions

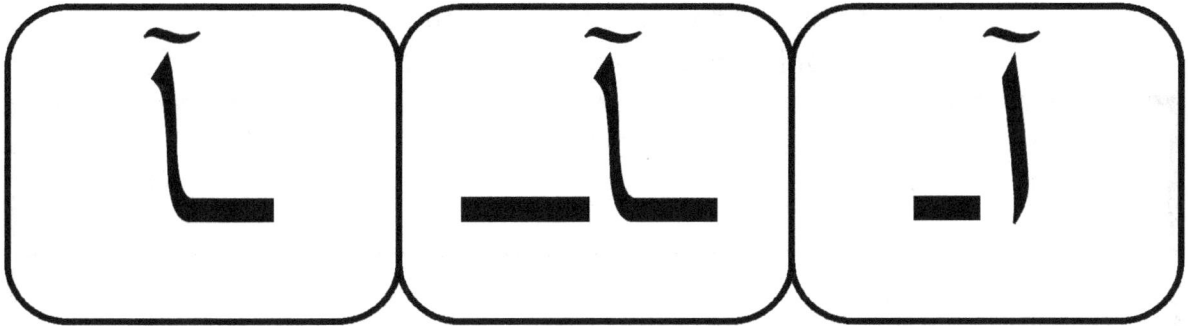

ٓ ـ   ـ ٓ ـ   ـ ٓ ـ

Stand-Alone and Beginning Forms

'Aalif-madda looks just like a regular 'Aalif with a little potato-chip tilde balanced on top.

1. First draw the 'Aalif as a single full-sized stroke. It starts a full height above the line, and goes <u>down</u> straight to touching the line.

2. Next, draw the tilde on top. It must be horizontal, not tilted. It should be balanced evenly left and right. It goes up a little bit, then down a little bit, just like our tilde. It rides the 'Aalif, going above the full height of text. Don't let it touch the 'Aalif, and don't let it get too far away so that it's not riding on top. 'Aalif is unconnected on the left.

Middle and Ending Forms

1. You're coming in from the line on the right side.

2. Draw the middle or ending 'Aalif going <u>up</u> after a curving corner. It goes up the full height of the line.

3. Draw the little tilde balanced on top of the 'Aalif. Because it rides on top, it's going to rise above the full height of the text. It's just a little potato chip--don't draw it too big. It's about the same size as a fatHa.

'Aalif does not connect on the left, so start the next letter over, after a small space, for the beginning and middle forms.

Writing Practice

Say the name of the letter, and make its sound,
each time you write the letter.

Writing Practice

Here we are cheating a little bit
with using generic bars to represent "other letters".
Since 'Aalif is unconnected,
a Beginning (or Middle) Form is
always followed by a Beginning Form.
Please do the practice anyway.

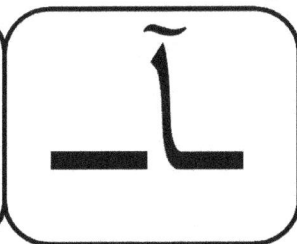

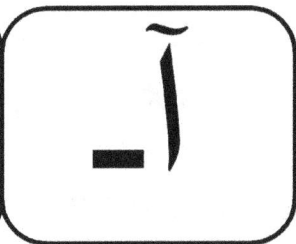

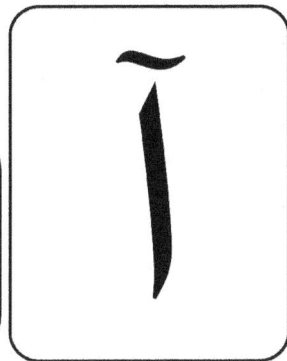

آ	ـآ	ـآ	آ

Know The Difference!

Stand-alone 'Aalif by itself has no potato-chip on top.	ا
hamza + 'Aalif is just a simple Hamza combination. It is pronounced " 'a ". It might have a Fat-Ha above it.	أَ أ
hamza BELOW the 'Aalif is pronounced " 'i ". It might have a KasRa below it.	اِ اِ إِ إ
hamza above the 'Aalif with a Dam-ma is pronounced " 'u ".	أُ
hamza by itself is simply a glottal stop. It's the silence in the middle of saying "Uh-oh!".	ء
If the potato-chip comes over the 'Aalif in a Laam-'Aalif L.A., then the "ah" is pronounced extra-long, just like before.	لآ

Reading Practice

آسِيا

A y i s ~A

ʿaasiyaa

Asia

آب

b ~A

ʿaab

August

آيس كريم

m y r k s y ~A

ʿaaees kreem

ice cream

القرآن

n ~A r Q L A

al-Qurʾaan

The Qurʾan

'aalif-maQSuurah

ى

aa

ـى

"long low back vowel"

أَلِف مَقصورة

The 'aalif-maQSuurah is actually a special 'aalif that is pretending to look like a Yaa', without the two points. So it is pronounced just like a regular 'aalif--"aah". It gets used for feminine words.

a

aa/a/ā

'aalif maQSuurah

is the Snake Without Wheels saying "Aaah"

Aaah! Water!
Sarah MacSurah, Irish snake,
At the end enjoys her break.
Happy snake no longer skates
Quiet peaceful bath she takes.
Underwater interlude
A-ppreciation A-ttitude.
Aah!

Helpful Hints

'aalif-maQSuurah is drawn just like a yaa', except without the two dots underneath. It is an unusual letter that indicates a feminine ending. Apparently the normal 'aalif was not fancy enough, so they wanted to make something more artistic.

Of course the normal yaa' (y) is pronounced "ee" (ii), whereas the 'aalif (A) is pronounced "aah" (aa).
So it's important to figure out which one it is that you're looking at.

Just in case this isn't enough, you probably remember that there is *another* irregular rule that says that when a hamza appears on a yaa', the yaa' loses its two dots.
Remember, **"the hamster takes the skates of snakes."**
However, it is still a yaa'!
So you have to remember that a snake without dots and with a **hamza** is still a **yaa'** ;
but a snake without dots and with **no** hamza
is in fact **'aalif maQSuurah**--the 'aalif that looks like a yaa'.

That should keep it exciting for you!

Q. Why is St. Patrick the patron saint of engineers?
A. Because he created the first worm drive...

142

Now You Sketch It--Doodles!

How To Write It

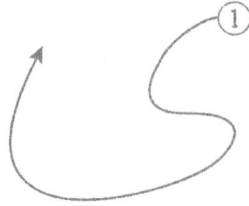

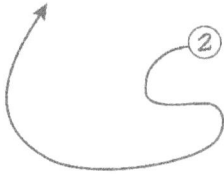

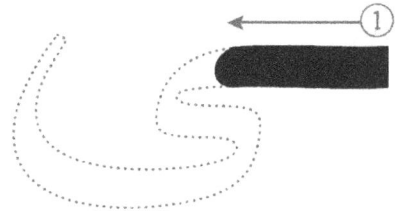

ى

Writing Suggestions

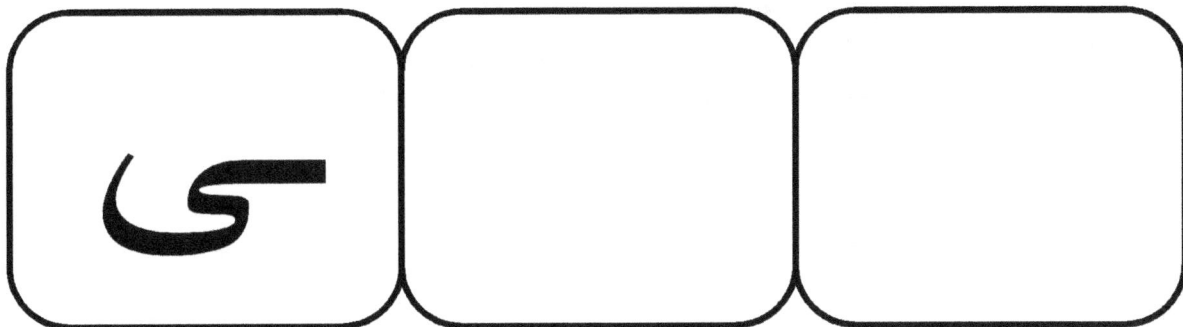

Stand-Alone Form

The stand-alone form looks like a yaa' without its dots. Draw a big swooping S-shaped curve. It looks like a snake starting to get out of a hot spring or a bathtub. Draw the head peeking up as one arch, then a flat place for the body where the body is floating on the surface of the water; then a big long tail that goes under the water and comes out pointing up on top. Make it artistic. Notice that the bottom part is *not* the same full bowl that we saw on noon, Sod/Dod, or seen/sheen-- it's slanting, pulled up to the surface on the right side, and so only finishes the bowl shape on the left.

No Beginning & Middle Forms

Ending Form

1. Come in on the line.
2. Overshoot just a little bit. That's the head. Then come back around, and draw a short, flat section left-to-right under the line. That's the snake's body. Then draw a big, long tail that comes down, goes back under everything, and sticks up again. This time the tail section is horizontal, not slanted like the Stand-Alone version. The bowl shape is flattened. The end of the tail barely peeks up above the line.

Writing Practice

Say the name of the letter, and make its sound,
each time you write the letter.

Writing Practice

'Aalif maQSuuRah has no beginning nor middle forms.
You could practice writing words from the reading practice
if you wish.

			ى
ى			

Know The Difference!

Yaa' the Yippee Happy Yelling Snake on Yellow Funny Roller Skates has two roller-skate wheels underneath. It is pronouced "ee" (like "y").

ي

When a hamza is surfing over a Yaa', the snake loses its skates but is still pronounced "ee". This is another special case.

ئ

noon has Nice Norman geNie's Navel above his big stomach.

ن

Ending Sod, the Sad, Sod Sand dune, has the Sand dune shape to the right.

ص

seen, the Silly Spectacles, (has Sue seen?) has wavy eyeglasses and a handle.

س

baa', taa' and thaa' all have a banana-boat, toboggin, or thawing-dish shape. These shapes sit on the line, and do not go below.

ب
ت
ث

Reading Practice

رأى

A ʻA r
ra'aa
to see, to think

يرى

A r y
yaraa
to see

أرى

A r ʻA
araa
I see

على

A L ª
ªlaa
on, at

صلى

A L S
Sallaa
to pray

Congratulations!

You have faithfully completed all of the exercises in the book--and if you've done all three books, the **entire course** in standard Arabic letters. You are now a new person!

> "The mind, once expanded to the dimensions
> of larger ideas, never returns to its original size."
> Oliver Wendell Holmes

To certify your accomplishment, we are here including a "Certificate of Completion" for you.

If you have an instructor, or if there is someone else who is teaching the course for you, you can have them sign your certificate for you.

If you're teaching the course to yourself, sign the certificate yourself after you've completed all the exercises and you know you deserve it.

Why not carefully tear your certificate out of the book, and post it on the wall where you can see it. It will remind you to be proud of your accomplishments. This will help focus your mind, so that you will become even stronger and more successful. Go for it!!

Certificate of Completion

This is to certify that

_____

has successfully completed

Week 3

Actually Learn Arabic Letters

and is fully entitled to receive all the benefits thereof

from this day onward

all through life.

Awarded this day

_____
date of achievement

_____
Signatory Authority

"The bold fonts make the letters easy to read. And the creative illustrations make the letters easy to remember. It's a fun and easy way for anyone to learn the Arabic alphabet."

Wendy Radwan, UCLA student

"I can't believe how interesting this is! It's not boring at all! The way the pictures stick in your mind, somehow it made me just want to keep reading it. And I found myself recognizing letters in the reading practice after only a few seconds of looking at the pictures. I couldn't believe it. This is the best course in learning Arabic letters I've ever seen. Anyone who needs to learn Arabic definitely needs to get this course."

Cora Mamerto, housewife

Go ahead and check out
http://www.authoritybooks.com/arabic.html
for some free stuff that will help you out.

AUTHORITY BOOKS, INC. AUSTIN, TX

www.ingramcontent.com/pod-product-compliance
Lightning Source LLC
Chambersburg PA
CBHW081329090426
42737CB00017B/3065